"This weekend I traveled back in tim[e]
reading this poignant and haunting mem[oir]
prose, Sandy Munro gives us an adult chi[...]
of the love affair between his mother, Betsy, and his father, Uri,
who never returned from the war. With 190 newly discovered letters,
Sandy takes a leap into the unknown, and the result is a remarkable
story of enduring love and bravery. Highly recommended."

—J. CARSON BLACK, AUTHOR OF
DARKNESS ON THE EDGE OF TOWN AND THE SHOP

"The lost father! A theme as American as apple pie, though in
Sandy Munro's case the quest is literal. In sturdy, straightforward
American prose Sandy tells the story of recovering vital information
about the father who died before his son had the chance to get to
know him. This occurs as a result of receiving almost two hundred
letters, an incalculable gift nobody could hope to receive. When Sandy
slits open the sealed shoebox, he detects 'a little puff of old attic
smell' and bends down to peer inside. What he finds there is more
than correspondence. It is the story of a man's life, and that of his
wife and son, forged in war and tempered by tragedy straight out
of the pages of history. I don't know how Sandy manages to create
suspense in a story whose ending is foreknown, but he does. Along
the way he discovers the truth every memoirist knows: writing is
remembering, and memory is unstable. "Maybe I don't remember
this at all," he writes. "Maybe it's only a dream." But the letters,
the real precious unaccountable box of old-fashioned handwritten
letters, argue otherwise. Read this book. It is touching, and true."

—KURT BROWN, POET AND FOUNDER OF
THE ASPEN WRITERS' CONFERENCE

"Sandy Munro's Finding Uri is a riveting and compelling story
that draws the reader in from the first pages on as he attempts to
unravel the unknowns and the mysteries surrounding who his father
was. While a personal memoir, it is also a fascinating and informative
historical journey that is easy to relate to but unique in its structure."

—BROOKE NEWMAN, AUTHOR OF *THE LITTLE TERN AND*
JENNIEMAE & JAMES: A PORTRAIT IN BLACK & WHITE

"A sense of decency pervades this fresh, well-written memoir
of family and war: there's a feeling that Sandy Munro is a good man
speaking from the heart about meaningful lives. Finding Uri is a
wonderful piece of storytelling."

—CLIFFORD IRVING

People's Press
Minds Wide Open

PUBLISHED BY PEOPLE'S PRESS

Post Office Box 70 • Woody Creek, Colorado 81656
www.PeoplesPress.org

Library of Congress Control Number: 2011925507
ISBN: 978-1-936905-91-1

Typeset in Baskerville, Professor, and Dakota Handwriting
Printed in the USA
Written by Sandy Munro

Dedication

for Alex, Sophia, Tommy,
and Uri

Introduction

He was the father I never knew, and so I don't know at all what to expect.

I have this one fleeting memory—it has to be from 1944, when I was three years old. We're in our backyard in Columbus, Ohio. I see brown creased trousers, a white shirt with long sleeves rolled up, a big smile, tanned high forehead, and short curly dark blond hair. He's brought home two balsa wood gliders and we're throwing them in the wind. He shows me how to hold the plane—two fingers pinching the fuselage below the wings—and aims for the center of the yard. The very first launch catches a big gust and the glider disappears high over the house. We're laughing, and maybe I don't remember this at all. Maybe it's only a dream, but I like to think that I remember it and that this is the way it was. Until now, it is the only time I can imagine being with him—and I can still see the plane, flying suddenly away.

A few months after Mom died, I received a box in the mail from her husband, Ted, whom she'd married ten years before. He had been gathering up her belongings and mailing them off to me piecemeal, so I didn't think much about it. The package, about the size of a shoebox, sat around for a week before I got around to opening it. One day I picked it up, slit the edge with my penknife, and felt a little puff of old attic smell as I peered inside. There were one hundred-ninety loosely packed letters—back and forth between my parents, Uri and Betsy, during my father's naval service in World War II. Many of his were mailed from his training base at Barbers Point, Hawaii, or later from the *USS Enterprise*, where he flew with Torpedo Squadron 90 during the last stages of the war in the Pacific.

The first thing I could think to do was to buy a fireproof lockbox. I had been given a rare gift that I had no idea existed—a chance to get to know my father—and wanted nothing to happen to the letters. I read only two when the box first arrived, one from Uri, and one from Betsy. I held off for almost a year while I decided how to approach them, and now it's time to start reading the rest. I don't really expect to learn much about the missions he flew. All the envelopes are stamped by the naval censor, and there won't be much about the war itself, but to read his words and imagine him writing them will be enough to connect me. It's been killing me to delay all this time, but I didn't know what to do. In recent weeks I began to feel that I should put down my thoughts as I read the letters. I could research his squadron's role in the war, and try to put the story together in something resembling real time.

Somehow I feel apprehensive about beginning. What will I find? I do know that in the single letter that I read from Uri, I saw a reflection of myself. I too was at sea aboard an aircraft carrier, separated for months at a time from my young wife and son, tied to them only by the letters we mailed to each other. Every letter meant the world to me, and from the one I read from Uri so far, I can see that he felt exactly the same. You're at sea with your squadron of brothers—living, breathing, and fighting for the life of the world you believe in, but it doesn't take you to the core and reason for it all. It doesn't take you home.

Uri

Most of the letters are from Uri. Then there are twenty-six more, still sealed, dated in January and February 1945. They're from Betsy, but he never had a chance to read them. The *Enterprise* was in the thick of the Pacific war by that time and mail deliveries were sporadic.

I've only looked over the envelopes, and a few of the letters which aren't in envelopes, in an attempt to get them in chronological order. What comes through at a glance is the devotion Uri showed my mother, and the tremendous strain of the separation on both of them. They tried to hide it by not talking about it and not thinking about it too much, but it's all there, in every page.

I'm well into the letters of 1943 now, and Uri has not yet joined his squadron. In May he was sent to Fort Schuyler Reserve Officer Training Corps in the Bronx for his initial naval training. Fort Schuyler was built in the 1840s in the aftermath of the War of 1812 to protect the western end of Long Island Sound, and hence New York Harbor, from attack by sea. It was shaped very much like the Pentagon, but with one flattened side, and lay at the edge of the Bronx where the East River meets Long Island Sound. Uri had left his new job as a chemical engineer in Princeton to volunteer for military service, and luckily was assigned to duty not too far from Betsy. She and I spent those four months with Alec and Barbara, Uri's parents, in Greenwich, Connecticut. I was a year-and-a-half old at the time, and my mother was twenty-one.

I spent today reading and taking notes. How strange to hear their voices in that time—the feel of their relationship, and their comments about me. Uri was five years older than Betsy, and his letters are filled with his daily activities. Like myself, he had to master Morse Code, semaphore (shipboard flag signaling), and the basics of military life necessary to an officer in the naval service. Most of it is easy enough but testing and competition are continuous, and low scores mean no weekends off to spend with his young family. Uri was trading watch-standing duties with fellow trainees in order to escape to Greenwich whenever he could.

Our family hasn't been separated at all until now, and they both seem careful not to talk about his immediate future, as he knows he's likely to be sent to the war zone. Like so many, that's why he joined up. For now, it's all about the adjustment of being apart for the first time, and their efforts to spend together whatever time they can arrange. Only four months after beginning officer training, Uri will be commissioned as an ensign in the US Navy.

September 9, 1943
7:00 p.m.

Darling –

You have just left, and when you left you took with you the most important part of me – all my love for you – without which my reason for being would be as nothing. Since we met you have meant all my happiness to me – and you always will, for as long as we are both here and perhaps even after.

Keep yourself safe, healthy, and as happy as you can, remembering we have a long big happy life together ahead of us, and we are going to enjoy it to the utmost – trying to make and keep each other happy all the time – doing things for one another and being nice to one another.

7

Goodbye for now, and take good care of little Stinker & let no harm befall him. All my love to you as always, Betsy darling.

x x x x x x x
x x x x x x x x   Love,
x   x   Uri

I am my father's only child, and I've wondered why my mother never mentioned the existence of these letters—but I'm beginning to get the idea. They contain the details of their daily lives, their financial worries, and even Uri's diagrams of how to drain and fill the car radiator with antifreeze. But mostly, they are love letters. She calls him "her daddy," and he refers to her as "mommy" or "old gal." Even during these short separations they find themselves lonely and are constantly reassuring each other of their love.

Today, as I was beginning to read the letters from 1944, I shared a few passages with my wife Mary Lynn. She pretends she isn't the old softy that I am, but she teared up immediately and told me that she just couldn't bear to hear any more. It's emotional stuff. To have it coming straight from the pen of my father puts us in real time in a way that I had not anticipated. Somehow, I'm right there.

It's sad. It wouldn't be that way if I didn't know how it all turns out. He's writing about their plans for the future, and always of his love for my mother and me, but he doesn't know how the real story unfolds. I have to try to lay that aside, and in my mind let them have their dreams while they can. I have to feel that same optimism, and not let it be shattered by the events that follow.

At first I couldn't figure out why there were no letters in 1944 until May, but it makes sense. They must not have been apart during that time. Uri had graduated from officer training school in New York in February 1944 and had not yet left for California to begin his aviation indoctrination. I know he and Betsy went to Corpus Christi and San Diego for his flight crew training, and that they were together in California before he left for Hawaii to transition to torpedo bombers. At this time, Mom and I moved back to her parents' home in Columbus.

I've only just started into the '44 series of letters, and there are a lot of them.

Random Notes on Mother's Day 1944

As Shakespeare might write it –
The moon shines bright, t'was on a night like this
A hope was born – a dream of better things to
*   come –*
A son, and heir – and all from Mother's womb!

As Ogden Nash might write it –
it's nice to have a luvver
it's swell to have a brudder
I'd rather have my mudder

As that great genius might write it –
Dear Mother " Me-Too "
We have a fine crew
Just Daddy and Sandy
and Betsy – Moo-Moo.

*   Versatile, ain't I?*
P.S. I am also good at card tricks and making love
to my wife.

*   U.*

I'm starting to key in to some funny similarities. I share my father's propensity for silly verse, which emanates from his own father, Alec. You'll hear more about this later, as Uri's father, whom I knew better than my own father, is a part of this story. Just the other day I found once again my dog-eared 1958 edition of *The Expert at the Card Table*, originally published in 1901. I carried the book aboard an aircraft carrier, the *USS Constellation*, for my senior summer cruise as a midshipman from the US Naval Academy. For two months in 1963, on our training cruise in the western Pacific, I spent hours at a time studying this mysterious book. It was written under the pseudonym S.W. Erdnase and reveals sleight-of-hand, card magic, and card-cheating techniques in great detail with masterful prose. It is truly the bible of card magic, and the author, perhaps for his personal safety, remains unknown. I've forgotten most of it, but there were a few years when I could put on a respectable card magic show. I can still do blind shuffles and card forces, but only well enough to fool an eight-year-old. Lastly, I'd like to think that I'm good at making love to my wife, but after forty-six years the jury may still be out on that one.

*

URI ALEXANDER MUNRO – 1944

It's October 1944 and Uri has joined his squadron. They're training in Hawaii in preparation for joining their ship, the *Enterprise*. Already more than a seasoned combat ship, she's the storied flattop of the Pacific. On December 7, 1941, she was 150 miles west of Pearl Harbor when the Japanese attacked. The next day she snuck into the devastated harbor for an overnight re-supply, and by December 9th she was steaming with a small task force in search of the enemy. They were in protection mode, patrolling the western approaches to the Hawaiian Islands—cycling in and out of Pearl Harbor every week or two for re-supply.

In June 1942, with her sister ship the *Hornet*, she helped defeat the enemy carrier navy in the Battle of Midway. By late October she was the last U.S. carrier still fighting in the Pacific theater. Of the *Hornet*, *Saratoga*, *Lexington*, *Yorktown* and *Wasp*, the *Saratoga* was the only other flattop still afloat, though she had been heavily damaged and would require repairs in Pearl Harbor. *"The Big E"* had taken six enemy bombs with more than three hundred casualties, but near the end of the year was sent to battle at Guadalcanal with the quickly repaired *Saratoga*. It had been a hell of a year for our Navy in the Pacific, but even worse for the Japanese. They never fully recovered from 1942, and the ship Uri would soon join was pivotal throughout the fighting.

At this point, he feels sure that he's going to be serving on the Enterprise, but he isn't able to confirm this information to Betsy.

October 20, 1944

I dreamed about you again - although it's vague in my mind now - partly - something about we were ski-ing, but we didn't have skis, just little red wagons like Sandy's. And then we went to a nice cozy cabin to get warm - - - -. It gets pretty bad when I dream about you at night as well as think of you all day, but I guess there is nothing I can do about it.

Goodnight sweetheart, or good morning, however you receive this, and all my love.

Uri

There's not much training time left at Barbers Point. Uri is a fanatical letter writer and sends six-page missives to Betsy almost every day. It's obvious that he worships her. He spends at least a page in every letter telling her how much he loves her, misses her, and how she's the sweetest and most beautiful girl in the world.

I know exactly what he was going through because of my own shipboard separations. There's a difference though. Uri knew he was going into battle, and I knew that I wasn't. Although I served during the Vietnam War, I was stationed on a ship in the Atlantic, outside the arena of combat. His experience had to be so much more intense.

It's especially painful to read the words about me, and what kind of father he wanted to be to me upon his return. I don't think I ever really understood just how devastating my father's loss was to my mother until now. He and I were the totality of her life. She was twenty-one years old, and had it all in front of her. Uri talks of how important it is to keep their life simple—that the little things are all that matter. He talks about cooking and washing the dishes with her. He mentions lying in bed, reading and listening to the radio with her. He reassures her that he wants nothing more to do with the military or flying airplanes after the war is over, and hopes to get back his old job in Princeton.

1944 doesn't seem so long ago, but little things in the letters keep illustrating how much times have changed. He talks about how there wasn't much to do in Hawaii. You could commandeer a jeep with some friends and take rides up into the mountains, and there were these amazing "water glasses" that you could take into the ocean and actually see fish all around you. I know that Jacques Cousteau had just invented the aqualung, but hadn't realized that swim goggles were a brand new development. At one point Uri asks Betsy if she might be able to find a pair of water glasses in Ohio or New York, but cautions her that they might be impossible to obtain. They were made of rubber, which like iron and steel was restricted for military use. He mentions that they might cost as much as six or seven dollars—likely prohibitive on their Navy budget. Meals at the military canteen were thirty-five cents for breakfast or lunch, and fifty cents for dinner. Uri complains about these high prices in Hawaii and that his meals were likely to cost seven or eight dollars more each month than he had anticipated.

October 25, 1944

The letters from you, and knowing that you are safe and well are an awful big help to my peace of mind, and I would go nuts without them, but it just isn't the same as coming home from after work, and watching you get dinner ready, and doing dishes with you and all the little things we do together all the time - such as stopping you in the middle of dishes and giving you a kiss and hug. Or having you sit on my lap and listen to the radio - or playing cards together, or just reading and looking over at one another. I think of all those things an awful lot, and it's because I love you so very much darling. We have had to live in so darn many places it will be nice to be in our own place again. I can't tell you how much I am looking forward to it all.

I have also been thinking about Sandy, and how hard I am going to try to be a good Daddy for him, and make him my friend and companion, as well as my son, & try to help and understand him. If I can do this I will be awfully happy. Goodnight now dearest, and pleasant dreams, with all my love,

Uri

Long before Uri joined his squadron, his new skipper-to-be, Lt. Russell Kippen, first appears in Edward Stafford's book, *The Big E*. It was early July 1943 while the ship was in dry dock for repairs and upgrades. The young lieutenant was out on a training flight with a passenger in the rear seat:

> *Once Lieutenant Russell "Kip" Kippen, feeling out an SNJ single-engine advanced trainer after hundreds of hours in Catalinas, rolled the J-bird over on its back after cautioning his back-seat passenger to tighten his seat belt, watched a chute blossom far below and called his passenger's attention to it, only to find that it was the passenger dangling beneath the chute, having fallen out of the J, seat and all.*
>
> — Edward P. Stafford, *The Big E*, p. 281

Kippen has just been named their squadron commander, and Uri feels honored to be "Kip's" radar/navigator. In those days, the skipper was only a lieutenant, but Kippen was a hardened pilot who had already served aboard the *Enterprise* in Torpedo Squadron Ten. In fact he had just returned from his last combat cruise flying the previous model Avengers from the deck of the *Enterprise*. They made the world's first nighttime carrier-borne attack on February 17, 1944, when they surprised the Japanese navy at the supposedly impregnable Truk lagoon and "wrecked the place," as reported by squadron historians.

The lagoon, north of New Guinea, was the forward anchorage of the Japanese fleet and the Japanese equivalent of our Pearl Harbor. Operation Hailstorm included three nights of bombing. Sixty enemy ships and 275 of their planes went to the bottom of the lagoon in seventy-two hours, and the attacks marked the end of Japanese sea power dominance in the Pacific.

Kip had completed his combat tour with Torpedo Ten and was expecting stateside duty, but the Navy found him indispensable and sent him back to command the newly commissioned Night Torpedo Squadron Ninety, (VT(N)-90). He was an inspirational hero to his new squadronmates. A more skilled and fearless leader was hard to imagine, and yet Kippen radiated calm.

Uri speaks with pride of Kip's flying skills. In addition to his flights with the skipper, he soon finds himself the designated training officer for all the new radarmen in the squadron. In the air his job is to navigate, operate the radar, and assist the pilot in the delivery of ordinance. This includes bombsight targeting as well as responsibility for the 30-caliber belly gun, which faces to the rear and downward. If the enemy has fighters in the sky, this gun becomes paramount, and it's the radar/navigator's job to use it. It requires Uri to climb out of his fold-up seat, turn around, crouch down, and face aft through the bubble.

The Avenger can attack ships at sea as well as targets on land. It carries either four 500-pound bombs, or two 1,000 pounders, or the deadly 2,000-pound Mark 13 torpedo. Or it could deliver a dozen 100 pounders, lay mines, and fire the new HVAR "Holy Moses" 5-inch rockets. It's an all-purpose, all-weather carrier-based bomber—specializing in low-level torpedo attacks.

Uri sends this note on my third birthday. We've been separated for about three months now and it's the first time we haven't been together for my birthday.

November 4, 1944

I'm glad to hear that Sandy is turning out to be such a smart little egg – just like his Mommy and Daddy. So he told his little friends that his Daddy knows God! That is quite a large order. However you can tell him that God is watching out for him and his Daddy & Mommy too...

...Yesterday I had a long hard day, and then had to get up at 1200 midnight & go out & do some bombing until 0400 in the morning, which is the main reason that I didn't get

to write. Right after dinner I went to bed to get a little rest. I'm going to bed real early tonight too, since I have to get up again at 0300 in the morning & get to work. These hours are really rough, believe you me.

I really don't mind night flying a bit, since I only go out with the very best of pilots. It isn't bad at all once you get used to not seeing anything. I am always busy in the air since I am generally in the lead plane in my practice attack, and I keep a lot of notes on what goes on so I can write up some kind of a report, among other things.

FATHER AND SON – THE ONLY PHOTOGRAPH

Time for deployment is coming up quickly and Uri is busy training and flying, but he still finds time for letters, a little tennis, chess, and even the occasional bridge match. There are parties every week or two, a Saturday night dance, and illogical amounts of beer and liquor to consume. It's amusing to hear my father writing about the girls at the dances. The Officers' Club would scour the islands looking for female

15

candidates to attend, and the single guys would draw straws choosing their dates—none of whom, Uri points out, come close to measuring up to his girl back home. More than once he mentions the bands composed of "colored boys" from the base, and how good they are. Some evenings the young officers would gather around the bands and sing songs for hours. Other times they would borrow a record player and spend the night playing records while writing their letters home.

Uri and Betsy try to keep each other informed of the little events in their lives each day. They would send their spending budgets and bank account details as well as mutual advice on all matters. They both smoked, and I notice one of Betsy's budget items is her weekly carton of cigarettes. Uri evidently enjoyed a few beers or cocktails, but considers himself a teetotaler compared to many of his squadron mates. In one of his letters he is obviously a little over the edge, but he was more likely to help drag his compatriots home from the O-Club than to be the problem himself. He has a liquor allowance in his budget along with everything else, and can't afford to exceed it.

*

It's another thing we have in common. I'm starting to see that we both like time alone—time to read, and time for music. Uri, like myself, is social to a point, but only so far. Twice he expresses frustration at not having time to read, but that he is trying to make room for it. I would occasionally hang out and play cards in the officers' wardroom, but more often found myself back in my little shipboard compartment totally engrossed in the guitar and banjo. Most of the time I'd play alone, but I'd always be scouting around for someone else to play with. Preferably someone who liked folk music and bluegrass.

My last two years aboard the *USS Wasp* ended in late 1968 and during that time my two best friends and fellow musician/bandmates were able to talk the naval personnel officer in Washington, DC into assigning them to the *Wasp* for their final tour of duty. John Sommers, Cash Cashman and I had met and formed a band in Pensacola, Florida, together while we were going through flight training three years before. Now we were playing music aboard an aircraft carrier. Our band was *The Clark County Coon Catcher's Quartet*, with the fourth member being Cash's blonde string-bass, which he named Sydney. We put on shows for the ship's company and became the informal musical mascots of the *Wasp*.

The skipper of our ship, Captain Ben Tate, was from Kentucky, and a bluegrass fan. We needed a place to practice, and so he gave us a key to Secondary Con. This was a large space, just under the flight deck, right in the bow of the ship. There were four portholes looking straight ahead sixty feet off the water, and a complete duplication of all the controls necessary to command the ship in the event the primary bridge was destroyed in combat. There were radar units on stands, another giant helmsman's wheel, and the engine order telegraph (EOT), which sent messages directly to the engine rooms below decks. We had the place all to ourselves as we practiced our tunes, one of us often sitting in the huge leather captain's chair. It was surreal to be playing folk music on guitars, bass and banjo while the *Wasp* plowed through the waves and aircraft were catapulted over our heads. At Christmas time in 1969 when I left the Navy, Cash and John followed Mary Lynn and me out to Colorado, where we've all been playing music ever since.

Uri didn't play a musical instrument, and he wasn't yet at sea, but music, one way or another, keeps popping up in his letters. Mom always stayed close to music. She always had a piano, and later in Maryland found and restored a beautiful antique pump organ. I remember that when I was young she loved to play and sing old church hymns. She'd have me sitting on a little footstool, pumping away on the pedals while she belted out the tunes. By the time I started school, I was learning to read the labels on my parents' record collection. I was careful with the records as I listened to them over and over again, sounding out the titles printed on the old 78s. There were Broadway collections, pop standards, hymns and classical pieces. Later, when I was in high school, Mom completely lost her singing voice from cigarettes, but still sat down and played the hymns or her thundering rendition of Chopin's Polonaise in A flat. I'd almost forgotten about much of this until now.

*

I have the advantage of being able to read the letters and follow the squadron's history in parallel time. The commissioning and training of Torpedo Squadron 90 took place from September to December 1944. Lt(jg) Robert B. Hadley, one of the pilots, documented the daily activities of the men as they prepared to embark aboard the *Enterprise*. His chronicle, which I found on the web, is an inside look at squadron life, the friendships, the ups and downs, and it affords me a bird's eye view of information that Uri was unable to communicate in his letters.

The censors had even outlawed "x"s as kisses in letters on the grounds that they could contain coded messages. Hadley's lively writing is fun to read. He catches the humor and spirit of a squadron training hard with the certain knowledge that they were the best in the world. His day-by-day account is not only riveting, but full of the human emotion that pervaded their impending departure:

> "From the outset, 90 showed the rugged spirit of the 'pioneer'. The charter members immediately laid the groundwork of the massive fortification at BOQ [Bachelor Officers' Quarters] "Dog" where eventually huge stockpiles of essential materials were amassed, all for the better and relentless campaigns at Barbers Point. But wait—we're getting ahead of our story. Actually, when 90 first arrived at BOQ "Dog," that lovely romantic two-story frame structure was the symbol of rural tranquility. Its spacious rooms, thickly carpeted parquet floors (decks, in case you USNRs don't understand) were linked by an intricate maze of winding, marble staircases (ladders). The antique furniture—some dated it back to prehistoric times —could not have been more unique. The mattresses were of rare vintage—in fact, the opinion was expressed that only the chow could claim priority in rank. Whatever the truth of these questions may be, 90 lived happily and lustily at BOQ "Dog" from September until the date in December (the 24th: "Twas the day before Christmas and all through the night there was ... bitchin'") when it went aboard the mighty Enterprise. Nor must we forget the strategic location of "Dog," just spitting distance from the Officer's Club where the Planter's Punch and Mike Jennings' double old fashions often made us feel almost as primitive as our surroundings.
> WELL ... such were the early beginnings!!"

— from Lt.(jg)Robert B. Hadley's VT(N)-90 squadron history

While their training took place at Barbers Point, the men lived in the bachelor officers' quarters described by Hadley. Along with full wartime training, the squadron found itself having to scavenge the fleet for its airplanes. Numerous configurations of the Avenger existed and they all had to be cannibalized and modified until they conformed to the TBM-1D version required for night missions. While the maintenance crews were salvaging parts from older TBMs and various decommissioned and crashed airplanes, the pilots trained in SNJ Texan trainers—a far cry from the more substantial birds to which they would soon transition. The squadron was supposed to be issued twenty-seven new planes, and forty pilots to fly them. One month before embarkation they had only eight planes, and almost none of these with the ninety-nine modifications required for night ops. It was with superhuman effort on the part of the squadron's maintenance team that on December 24th the pilots flew aboard the *Enterprise* with twenty-four night-ready TBMs.

This latest Grumman Avenger TBM-1D was the first aircraft designed for night carrier operations, and the first all-weather carrier-based bomber. Accidents were common during night landings, and the history of Uri's squadron is full of them. Six squadron mates were lost in training off Barbers Point before they had a chance to join the *Enterprise*. The TBM, with its fifty-four foot wingspan and nineteen hundred horsepower Wright radial engine, was a hog. It was forty feet long, prop to tail, almost eight feet longer than the F6F Hellcat fighters that would join them aboard the ship. Designed to operate at thirty thousand feet, it could make almost three hundred knots straight and level. The crew of three included the pilot, radar/navigator, and rear gunner. The aircraft later achieved fame as the model flown by Lt. George H. W. Bush when he was shot down in the Pacific, and even more famously when five TBMs were lost near Florida in the original "Bermuda Triangle" incident. All the same it was a good aircraft: stable because of its large wing surfaces, and designed to float if unintentionally landed on water. Not that it was anything like a seaplane—a water landing was not generally an intentional event.

My own last fourteen months in the Navy were spent flying T-28s. The Trojan was also a radial-engined aircraft and at first glance could be mistaken for an Avenger, but was three-fourths the size. I taught formation flying in the training command in Pensacola and often checked out a plane on the weekend for solo "having fun" flights. It took full right rudder to counteract the engine torque on take-off. Without it, you would spin off the runway to the left as you jammed the throttle forward. That was the first thing you learned about a big single-engined radial. I flew the same side number every day, and that plane soon became an old friend. Every sound was familiar and the plane felt like an extension of my own body in the air. These weekend flights usually had some upside-down time as well as mock dogfights with OV-10 pilots from nearby Eglin Air Force Base. The throaty rasp of my engine and raw power of 1,450 horsepower on the runway made me think of my father and the strangely similar experiences we inadvertently shared. First the airplane itself, but also shipboard life and the camaraderie of the squadron. It's not hard at all for me to visualize the life he was living.

*

The three-and-one-half months at Barbers Point were crammed full. The VT(N)-90 crews were flying at night, mostly from midnight until dawn, while other squadrons living in BOQ Dog were on a daytime schedule. Since the men were spread throughout the two-story barracks, there were constant battles over sleep disruption. Everyone needed time to unwind, party and listen to their record players, but the two squadrons were on opposing schedules. Things were partially solved by having all the TBM crews move to the second deck, left wing.

Uri talks of drunken brawls, walls being kicked in, and broken glasses on the floor. At one point some of the VT-33 members down the hall had been keeping the "90" boys awake with their partying. A few of them were on the chubby side and Uri and his mates went down to their rooms with pillows under their shirts singing, *"The boys from VT-33, so fat they cannot see their pee."* The battles escalated until Uri and his pals went into the rooms when the VT-33 boys were out, turned over their beds, emptied their drawers, took their doors off the hinges, threw them away, and nailed their closet doors shut.

As it turns out, every squadron needs to function as its own loyal brotherhood, and these clashes played a necessary part in building the cohesiveness that the times would soon require.

November 30, 1944

There was sort of a wolfing game in progress between the single men who had dates and those who didn't. Most of the married ones with 2 or 3 exceptions didn't bother with the gals but stuck to drinking and singing songs. I don't see anything particularly wrong in dancing with them, but just sitting there I can't help mentally comparing them with you, and whenever I do that and think of you I just don't have any more interest. I sure must have changed since marrying you, darling. When you're not around, a party just isn't the same thing to me. Really it is kind of funny, I can't really explain it, but being away, logically you'd think that you would feel more lonesome, and have more of a desire for feminine companionship, but it doesn't seem to work out that way with me. I probably would pay more attention to the feminine factor with you right there, but when you're not there it changes everything. I have tried to be very frank and tell you how I feel sweetheart, but it doesn't make very good sense. I'm afraid it is an acute case of love, which is the hardest thing in the world to explain logically. Darn it here I am in the 6th page, & not thru. Will finish tomorrow. For now remember this – I loved you the moment I saw you, and have always loved you since then, and always will, and all I will ever need is your true love for me. If I have that I will never lack for anything because that is all I need. Love me always darling, and help me, because I always lean on, and count on your love perhaps more than even you realize.

Always, Uri

I know exactly the feeling Uri expressed. Some men feel liberated away from their wives and could easily establish liaisons with the ladies. Somehow I found myself self-conscious and introspective in that situation. I couldn't just play the boy-gets-girl game. I might have had fantasies about it, but could never act them out. It wasn't even so much a moral objection as a feeling that would come over me, much as Uri described it.

I just found this out-of-place note from early December.

December 4, 1944

ODE TO A FAIR LADY

Mae West has bosoms large and ample
Dietrick's legs are but a sample
Lovely Grable has her points
Gypsy Lee her lissome joints
But you, my love, are up to snuff
Of what is necessary, you have enough!

Your wondering and loving,
Uri

I can see that there will be some chronology confusion in these letters. There are only a few from Betsy during this earlier time period. She may not have kept them, and they haven't turned up.

He's a playful dad, as I'm discovering. It makes me wonder whether I could retrieve any of my time with him through hypnosis. I am getting a better feel for his personality, which brings him closer, but so far I cannot see and feel him in my mind's eye.

Betsy

It's starting to feel like, in a way, I've gone wrong. The idea was to get to know my father—and now I find that I don't know my mother very well at that time in her life. I'm intimate with the older version, who raised our family in Maryland and became a civil rights crusader in the late '50s, but have a hard time interpolating backward to her early years with my father.

The intensity of her personality may become more apparent as I read. I have no doubt simplified her to the attractive young mother with nothing on her mind but her little son and her husband at sea. From her earlier letters, before Uri joined his ship, it was obvious she was dreaming ahead to their life after the war. She thought of this period as an interruption to their real life, but a time that would come to an end. The war was an anomaly—not what anyone could have imagined, but a time to be endured.

Betsy was born Elizabeth Dorcas Magnuson in Columbus, Ohio in June 1921. She had four brothers; three older, and Ted the younger. I knew them all, but especially Ted. The older brothers were in the Army, and missing from my earliest years. Ted was the hilarious teenager in the house, and my best friend when Uri was away. Mom and I lived with her parents in Columbus a good part of that time. A respected upper middle-class family on Ardmore Road in Bexley, they were good solid Ohio Swedes, one generation removed.

Betsy had plans to go to Ohio State until she was introduced to Uri by her brother Bill. Uri was a chemist and assistant plant manager for the Frey-Yenkin Paint Company in Columbus. We don't have to imagine much about the love between them. We have a few pictures, and now the letters. By most standards, my mother was a looker. Five-foot-two, blonde, and yes—eyes of blue. Uri was a Dartmouth graduate, class of 1937. He was five-foot-seven, athletically inclined, and a member of the ski team and the chess club. He was an intense debater— fast to laugh, and quick to rebut. I know that he had a jealous nature and was capable of boiling over.

Mom used to tell us the story of three guys in a car behind them in traffic. They had yelled out, "Hey blondie, why don't you ditch that guy and come with us?"

Without a word, Uri jammed the gearshift of his convertible into reverse, floored the car, and smashed full power into their car behind him. Then he leapt out of the car to go after them. They pulled around his car and drove off in a panic, water draining out of their radiator.

Until the letters, my only knowledge of my father came from dinner table stories, and what I gleaned from the sparse collection of photographs that Mom left behind. I sensed that it remained difficult for her to talk about him in any depth, and so it became a topic that we both consciously avoided. I do know that in the two years before the war he became another member of the Magnuson family. There were football and baseball games in the field down the street, and card games most nights. It was a house of raucous brothers, and one sister who could obviously hold her own.

Uri and Betsy were married on February 8, 1941, evidently a noteworthy social event as illustrated by *The Columbus Dispatch*...

Columbus Sketches . . By WILL DANCH

"We're going to have to postpone our wedding. Uri Munro bought that beautiful ring we were admiring in the jeweler's window for his bride!"

The couple was first separated when Uri left for Fort Schuyler for his officer-training program, but then re-united again for a while in Corpus Christi and San Diego. When Betsy wrote this letter, they had been married two-and-one-half years.

June 17, 1943

My dearest Uri,

I'm sitting here waiting for you to call. Honest Uri I wish it would ring soon as I can't wait to hear your voice. I miss you more and more every day. I'm happy all right Uri and of course the baby gives me something to do but I'd give a million to have you with me. You're such a darn sweet daddy and you mean the world and all to me. Tears start rolling down my face and I can hardly see the page. Forgive me Uri but I know you'll understand. It just amounts to the fact that I'm only half living when my daddy is away from me.

June 22: She's seeing him most weekends, but writes ...

training pants – 4 pr.	2.00
stationary	1.00
stamps	.73
groceries	.75
	4.48

Cigarettes and a few other things have left me with about a dollar or so.

I love you darling with every little bit of me. I already dream of the war ending and our starting up again. I'm going to be a better than ever wife. Take care of yourself darling.

Betsy

*

Uri doesn't go into great detail about his officer training, but I get the idea that Fort Schulyer was fast-tracking trainees to meet the high demands of the war effort. I tried to compare his military indoctrination to mine, but it's apples to oranges. I'm sure there was pressure, and a certain amount of hazing, but he never mentioned it in his letters. His entire officer-training program lasted four months, while my experience as a plebe at the Naval Academy lasted a full year, and was designed to weed out those who might crack under pressure. We were taught that you needed to be able to depend on your shipmates in battle and that the time to get rid of weak sisters was now.

As plebes, we were Fourth Classmen, and fourth-class citizens of the Brigade of Midshipmen. We were taking twenty semester hours in an engineering curriculum each quarter, lining up for inspections three times a day, marching in parades, playing sports, all the while being "trained" by any and all members of the three classes that were senior to us. Just maintaining uniform appearance was a major effort. We spent impossible amounts of time working on our shoes. Kiwi shoe polish, and endless small, light-touch circles with a rag dipped in water and stretched over your index finger did the trick. Anything less than a mirrored appearance was unacceptable.

Everything in your room had a designated location. Each shelf in your closet was assigned by diagram. The proper number of black, brown, white, and athletic socks—in the proper order. Underwear, folded properly, on the shelf below. Either you or your roommates could be inspected and reported for infractions by any upperclassman at any time.

Three times a day we sat at a table for twelve, with four plebes lining one side of the table. Immediately across from us were last year's plebes, now called Youngsters. A mix of First and Second classmen sat at each end. Plebes had to "brace up" at all meals by sitting on the edge three inches of the chair, back straight, eyes in the boat (straight ahead), chin tucked tight. We were not to speak unless spoken to. We passed the food and ate last, and someone who wanted to apply pressure to you could destroy you with "professional questions." You might be asked for a dissertation on Sumner Class destroyers for the next evening meal, and had to find a way to spend an hour out of the next twenty-four in the library and another memorizing your presentation. If your performance was deemed unsatisfactory, you'd be placed on report for Professional Questions, Failure to Answer. Being placed on report meant getting up at 0500 hours (instead of 0615), donning your sweat gear and doing calisthenics for an hour with other offenders under the supervision of a Marine drill instructor. Day after day of this, on top of everything else, could wear you down. We were reminded that nearly a fourth of all midshipmen were their high school class presidents, an equal number were valedictorians, and many were the sons of senior naval officers—themselves decorated Academy graduates. Flunking out wasn't like dropping out of college. It was a failure to uphold the family name.

At Annapolis, plebe year was designed to eliminate ten or fifteen percent of each incoming class who were unofficially designated as "fucked up." There was no real definition of this phrase, but it was assumed that we knew it when we saw it. If you didn't fit the mold, pressure was applied and sooner or later you'd be gone. Years later I began to believe that some of this was misguided. Battles at sea throughout history have been gruesome and bloody affairs. Heroism was common aboard Navy ships but you could seldom predict who would crack and who would perform. Certainly the young officers who were training with my father rose to the occasion when the battle began, and many had spent only a few months in officer preparation. I believe now that the Navy needs all types of personalities to do its best job. It needs measured and sensitive performance as well as two-fisted bravado.

*

They haven't yet begun the long separations. It's innocent stuff with lots of romantic teasing on both sides, and reminds me of the letters Mary Lynn and I wrote to each other when I was at sea. If anything, Betsy is the more forward of the two. I was too young at the time of course, but now I'm getting to see Mom as she was—giddy in love with this perfect man in her life. I'm an accidental interloper into my parents' lives at a precise moment in time. It's the moment that carved out our future. I just had no idea that it would feel like I was going through it all, with the two of them, in real time.

She is only twenty-two, and with hindsight I find myself trying to project the real life that was ahead of her onto her personality. But it hadn't happened yet. No two years of Uri being declared missing. No meeting the handsome young Army captain and paratrooper from the 82nd Airborne, and survivor of the war in Europe. No five kids, or the mini-farm in Maryland. No civil rights battle that eleven years later would end up in the U.S. Supreme Court. Right now she's just one of the many thousands of young mothers who are proud but terrified as their husbands go to war.

July 7, 1944

Sat. we will have a wonderful time. I'm going to buy a pint of gin and we can make some Paradise drinks. That's a good name for them because when my daddy and I are alone it is paradise.

At this point in some ways I don't recognize her. I don't see that intense personality. I don't see the crusader. I see a young mom biding her life until the moment when she can be with her man. She's practical. She's taking care of me, and she's sharing her life with friends. At one point she and three other Navy wives started a wood shop making hobbyhorses to be sold for Navy charities. I remember seeing a newspaper article with a photograph, Betsy reaching toward a wooden hobbyhorse with a little paintbrush. She's standing beside a bandsaw with the other girls and I wish I could find that picture now. It had to have been in Ohio.

It's early in October and we're back in Columbus, biding time until Torpedo 90 joins the ship. Betsy is all too aware that it won't be long. Only a few weeks before, they said their good-byes in San Diego. Betsy and I drove east while Uri flew to Honolulu to finally climb into the new TBM Avenger. Now his squadron would be spending three months getting to know their actual airplanes. I don't have many letters from my mother to Uri in 1944. He would have been receiving most of them in Hawaii and likely didn't take them aboard the *Enterprise*. He must have sent them home to her, but they haven't turned up.

Most of their conversations involve logistics and news, but they all contain the longing that was central to their feelings. It's Christmas 1944, and a lonely time for the Magnuson family. Betsy is sad to be at home, away from Uri and her brothers. With three of them fighting in Europe, her mother Clara is depressed. Her father's argumentative optimism about the war is "a pain in the neck" to both of the women.

Christmas Day 1944

You know Uri, it's rather funny, but I've always felt sorrier for the mothers of the boys, more so than the wives but today I changed my mind. In the first place, it's more obvious with the parents because they are older and can not adjust themselves but secondly and more important is the difference in the reasons why parents want the boys home in comparison to the wives reasons. Mother and Bern were talking today and the things they said made me feel so different about the whole thing. They want to see the boys finish their educations, getting married, having good parties like we used to, etc. We wives want our homes again, our partners in married life, fathers of our children, the guy who we can pour our hearts out to, and our lovers. There really is a great difference, it can't be measured or compared in many ways but on the other hand it's all the harder on we younger ones when we have to listen to their moaning and groaning about this and that. This is a very hard letter to write Uri because my emotions are so mixed. I'm thankful for so much, and happy because of many things. Thank God I can draw away from everyone and think only of the best. Christmas was ruined for me one hundred per cent, that is for me personally.

Sandy had a wonderful Xmas and was the most excited adorable little boy that I've ever seen all day long. He loves his table and chairs. I told him that you told Santa to bring them down and he tells everyone, "Look at this, Daddy told Santa to bring me this." He really seems to think more of it because you have something to do with it. It's surprising how much he talks about you Uri. He's always saying how much he loves and misses you.

I can't remember much from those early years, but the overwhelming feeling of my mother missing Uri stays with me. I'm looking now at the oil painting she commissioned in Columbus at the time. I vaguely remember that there were several long sittings. She's sad and beautiful in a soft, short-sleeved red dress. A jeweled, inverted triangular pendant glistens from the narrow neckline. I'm tucked in close to her left side in my sailor's suit—four years old, serious, looking like a little man already. I notice the Munro high forehead even then, as much above the eyes as the whole face below. Next to my leg is a little wooden giraffe standing on a red base and held upright with strings that are kept tight by a spring. Squeeze the bottom of the cylinder holding the spring, and the giraffe collapses as if shot. Though my mother's hand is in the shade, her wedding ring glows into the shadows.

We recently had the painting restored. It hangs high on the wall between two trusses across from me as I write these words, and is a treasure that changes continuously with the path of the sun through the clouds.

BETSY AND SANDY, 1945

I remember my mother talking about my father, and there was a long wait after he was declared missing. The two of us traveled much of that year-and-a-half before the Navy confirmed his death. We went to San Diego, back to Princeton, then settled for a while with the family in Columbus. There were friends in each place, and Mom wanted to stay in touch with them. Before the war, when we lived in Princeton and Uri worked at the chemical engineering firm, a frizzy-haired man in a shaggy grey sweater would wave to me in the yard when he walked by our house each morning. He lived just down the block, on Mercer Street, and his name was Albert Einstein. I don't remember this, but Betsy swore by it. Later, as a physics teacher in the early '70s I had a chance to tell my class about it. Even now it seems uncanny.

It's almost Christmas, and any day now, Uri will be flying aboard his new home. He's still not allowed to tell Betsy which carrier his squadron will be joining, although there are a limited number of possibilities. It's hard to imagine the enforcement of that level of secrecy when we compare it to our world today. She knows he's a member of Night Torpedo 90, but has no way to confirm which ship he'll be stationed aboard. The war is heating up as the last drive surges toward the Japanese mainland. The Philippines are almost back under Allied control, Formosa and Okinawa the last major enemy strongholds. Torpedo 90's crews are sure they'll be flying to Tokyo repeatedly before this cruise comes to an end.

It has been four months since Uri left for Barbers Point, and now—any day—he could find himself flying his first combat mission. Betsy somehow knows this, but her life is the same as it has been these past months. She's up and down, fearful one day, determined to persevere the next.

Alec

Getting to know my father through his letters makes so much more sense because I'm intimate with his upbringing. I know the surroundings, and I was tied strongly to his father. That's the other part of the story that I need to pass down the line. I was hoping to keep myself further removed from the narrative, but this process keeps bringing me back in. It's also a part of Uri's unique family story, and I'm the last person with a chance to tell it.

Uri's parents, his Scottish father and Russian mother, were resourceful people, raising a young boy in America. Uri's father, Alec, was the straight and true backbone that I'm starting to recognize in our family tree. We look alike, and it doesn't stop there. I wish he was here now. He'd be able to tell me more about Uri just when I'm finally ready to ask.

It wouldn't have made as much sense to ask what Uri was like before I began this project. I already know some of that, but he appeared to me as a sketch, only an outline. Mom often said that he was funny, he had a temper, he was loyal, he had a jealous side. Perhaps I could have asked for more stories, and this might have led me deeper. I didn't probe enough. I never knew that a time would come when I would need to know more. I'm now realizing that Uri's picture comes in so much clearer because of the thirty-three years I had with his father.

*

Alec was born in Thurso, Scotland in 1884. I have a picture of him when he played on the Russian Olympic soccer team in 1912, though he was a Scot through and through. It was the early, golden age of international business. Alec had gone to work in sales in Russia for an English tool manufacturer in Petrograd, and started playing football (soccer) with his new countrymen. He had already been a standout footballer and wrestler in Scotland. I know that he was elected captain of the Russian team and would have played again in the next Olympics had not the impending war cancelled the 1916 Games.

The team photo shows a small crowd and wooden bleachers on the field near a river. They're wearing white open-necked shirts, knee-length black shorts tied with drawstrings, and tall woolen socks. Funny though, standing there with their ankle-top leather shoes, there isn't a real smile anywhere. It's a tough-looking lot of young Russians out to win football games. "No time outs, no substitutions," Alec told me. He was seated in the center, looking perhaps the meanest of all, displaying the hereditary Munro frown. In pictures I've seen myself pulling my eyebrows down that way, as if I'm angry, when I'm not.

St. Petersburg team photo: Alec, seated center

Thurso is in County Caithness and is the northernmost town of mainland Scotland. From there you catch the ferry forty miles further to the Orkney Islands. When Mary Lynn and I visited Scotland in November 1991, we traveled northwest into the Highlands by car, then turned east and spent a few days "grave chasing," as the Scots like to call it. We found only one cemetery in Thurso. It was on a hillside overlooking the town. From there you could see Scrabster Harbour, beyond which ships crossed the Pentland Firth and passed the Orkneys on their way to the North Sea.

We parked the car in town and climbed the short hill to the iron-fenced meadow. The Munro family tombstone appeared almost immediately, with an engraving on the bottom that told us Alec and his brother John had been maintaining it all these years. We could see that flowers had been planted and had been in summer bloom. Some faded purple petals, perhaps cranesbill or mallow, had blown against the beautifully cut base of the dark marble gravestone.

As we read the inscription it was hard to imagine how these young Munros could have been taken at such a robust time in their lives. You'd think that the sluicing northern winds would have long ago inoculated the population. Now I've found a letter from Isabel MacCaig, my grandfather's niece, dated July 26, 1989. Isabel is the wife of Norman MacCaig, the poet, whom we shall get to know soon enough. She had written in response to my questions about her "Uncle Alec."

There were four brothers and two sisters in Alec's family. The father, Finlay, was a policeman and later the schoolmaster at the Thurso primary school. Isabel told me that son James was an apprentice joiner who died from a strangulated hernia. Both of the younger sisters followed only a month later, Mary from a perforated stomach ulcer, and Sallie from tuberculosis. Their brief story is etched in the stone, but the family deaths of 1906 defy emotional reason. It's hard to imagine how my great-grandmother Robertina survived her remaining two years. Of Alec's surviving brothers, John was Isabel's father, and Murdock Murray became a shipbuilder in Portuguese East Africa. They both died before their 70th year. Alec himself would live until a few days before his 94th birthday.

Isabel wrote to me ...

> *"Uncle Alec was a kind of fairy godfather who, with or without Uri, appeared from time to time bearing gifts and taking the whole family out for a sumptuous trip with sumptuous meals. Something else your grandfather may never have told you is that my father John was never able to "save" any money as my mother had always been subject to nervous breakdowns as they were then called. After he died at the age of 66 they became increasingly frequent and prolonged. Until she died eight years later Uncle Alec sent me 200 pounds (quite a lot of money in those days) to help pay for nursing home expenses."*

The wind picked up as we pulled our collars tight and walked down into town from the cemetery, looking for 36 Duncan Street. Evidently the residents of Thurso were tied closely enough to their homes to have their street address carved right there on the gravestone. Hundreds of years of fishing and slate quarrying defined the town nestled aside the steep hills of Dunnet Head. Many of the original foundations survive, including St. Peter's Church, begun in 1220, with its surprisingly graceful arches, but no roof. The woman who owned the town bakery told us that village hadn't changed much in the last forty years, and we suspected much longer. As we walked among the mostly buried foundations and shards of the Viking population that was driven from Caithness in the early 1200s, it didn't take long to find the Munros' house. I remembered a photograph in one of my grandfather's many scrapbooks in Greenwich. A low-to-the-ground seacoast stone cottage with an uneven slate roof—and now it was sitting before us.

We knocked on the door and were immediately invited in by James and Liz MacDonald, a couple in their sixties. They offered us scones and tea and told us that if we'd only arrived six months earlier, we'd have seen the house as it looked when my grandfather's family lived in it eighty years before. It was newly remodeled inside, but from the scrapbook photo you can see that the outside looks exactly the same. Along one side of the house is a tall stacked-rock wall that divides the narrow yard from the single-track road. There is no concrete holding the rocks together, and the wall totters, leans and swells out in places. All the same it was beautifully built and grew naturally out of the rocky landscape. Grandpa Alec had told me that he and his brothers had just finished the roof when the picture was taken. They'd laid up the pasture's stone fence by clearing the rocks from the fields adjacent to the house. He told me that every four or five years that they would have to clear the fields again as new rocks kept swimming their way to the surface, causing the fences to grow taller over time. I had no notion that rocks could somehow climb their way upward, but after years of collection building stone, I've observed it here in the Rockies as well. More likely it's an illusion. The disturbed soil slowly erodes, exposing more stone.

Although Grandpa was most interested in football and wrestling, he had every reason to pay attention to his studies as his father was the headmaster. "It was strict," he said. "There was no nonsense, mister. You were there to learn, and if you misbehaved, it would be a good, stiff rap to the knuckles." He was an incessant reader, and even in the last few weeks of his life was still spending time with his books. Two years before, I had asked him to write out as much of his family history as he could remember. He said, "I'll do it Sandy, but in my book, it's not where you've been, but where you're going that counts."

When I was five or six years old, Grandpa told me stories of his travels before the First World War. He had been a sailor in the British Navy and showed me his tattoos. One was a blue anchor, barely visible in the white hairs of his forearm. He pointed out another one on his other arm, but I couldn't really make it out. He had a tremendous sense of place, and an interest in the family origins of everyone he met. Origins told him something. He had traveled much of the world, and always connected people he met with their ancestry. We'd call it "profiling" now, but in Alec's time the world was much less homogenized. He felt he knew what to expect from an Italian, or a Russian, and his calculations were informed by the places he had been. He grew up in what he once told me was the true golden age of man. "Those were the best times of all. No war—and you could go anywhere in the world without a passport."

He married the beautiful Varvara Gansin, from a successful Petrograd family, and was moving up in the world in mid-1916 when Uri was born. Alec and his small family prospered in the rapidly changing, pre-revolutionary world they found themselves. The city of Petrograd was the jewel of northern Russia. Previously called Saint Petersburg, it became Leningrad in 1924 and is now Saint Petersburg again. My grandmother Varvara told stories of this beautiful city that came to have three different names in less than a hundred years, and it seems inevitable that I will go there someday. Alec described his week-long skiing trips in the countryside around Petrograd. Young and adventurous, he and his friends would set out with little food, but with the idea of staying in farmhouses and being fed by strangers. It was cold country, not far from the Arctic Circle, barely south of the lower tip of Greenland. It's still the northernmost city of over one million people on our globe.

In the cold Russian winter, three or four friends would ski the countryside a week at a time, dependent on rural neighbor hospitality. Alec was a barrel stave cross-country skier and his stories painted images for me of snow-covered roads and wide-open spaces with few trees. There were expansive stretches of farmland and miles to ski before the night. They'd follow the roads which carriages couldn't manage that time of year, and stay at whatever farmhouse they found themselves when evening came on.

It amazed me that Grandpa could still remember a family he'd met only once—the ingredients of their simply prepared meal, their son's name perhaps, and what the father did for a living. This from the years starting in 1909 and leading up to the Communist revolution eight years later. When asked how he kept all these things in mind, or how he knew so much, Grandpa would reply, "The Divil is not so smart Sandy, but veery, veery old."

With the revolution upon them the family escaped Russia by train early in 1917. The Bolshevik guards passed through the crowded car checking identification, and Alec and Varvara felt it necessary at one point to hide Uri in a suitcase. With Grandpa's memorabilia I found a letter that seemed to indicate that they crossed the border north of Petrograd with the help of a family friend, Bruno Barlach, who was a controlling officer in the Swedish army. Bruno arranged boat transportation to Tornea-Haparanda, at the northern tip of the Baltic Sea.

They would finally feel safe there on the Swedish-Finnish border. It was apparent that they were leaving Russia none too soon. The White Russian resistance was melting away, and the Bolsheviks were clamping their society down. My father had been born just in time to be chased out of his own land.

VARVARA AND URI, NEW YORK, 1919

They first settled in New York City and lived for a while near West 91st Street, where Uri attended the Trinity School. Three years later they moved to White Plains, before ending up in Greenwich, Connecticut. Eight years after they immigrated, Alec went to work for a successful new company, Northam Warren Corporation, the makers of Cutex nail polish and Peggy Sage cosmetics.

As airplanes began criss-crossing the oceans he became their export manager. It was his job to open the world to the company's product line. In doing so, he became fluent in French, Spanish, Portuguese and German as well as his second language of Russian. In the scrapbooks you can see him standing in his suit beside a Ford Tri-Motor in Borneo, or beside the Great Buddha in Kamakura. He spent years establishing South American markets for Cutex, and in his seventies and eighties was still visiting his Brazilian friends. Even in his nineties, after living in the United States for sixty years, Grandpa Alec's brogue was smudged thick. He used to say that he found it an advantage in business. When you went out into the world you found people who distrusted Brits, Germans, Russians, and even Americans, but everyone seemed to enjoy a Scot.

Although the scrapbooks depict a serious man with seldom a smile on his face, I know now that it was more about his stuffy sense of propriety when having his picture taken. In reality he was fun-loving, the natural life of any party, and a non-stop singer of jingles and poems from his travels. He would tell us their origins, and recite them at the dinner table in the appropriate language. When we asked what they meant, we'd get the often indecipherable Scottish translation—like this original Highlands tag line:

Eenty zeenty figgity fell

El del dominel

Arkie barkie tarry rope

Zeen teen tan toosh Jock... You're It!

After Uri was lost, my mother sent me for two weeks every summer to Greenwich to stay with my grandparents, until I graduated from high school. Varvara was Barbara now, but still spoke with a thick Russian accent. I remember as a little kid how I'd keep asking her to say the word "abracadabra." It came out more like "ardracabardra," and I thought this was hilarious. She was tiny, less than five feet tall, and with a dark complexion, which may explain my easy tan.

Grandpa and I would often walk the mile or so to the post office after breakfast. I traveled that route a few years ago and instantly had visions of balancing myself by holding his hand as I walked the top of the stone wall lining the sidewalk. We'd stop at the library, first to return his books, then continue on to Box 537 at the post office, then back up to the library to pick up the next batch. He'd have three or four: a mystery, a biography or two, and always a history book. He would sometimes pick up books that he had ordered in different languages. I would ask him to read them to me and he'd make a big show of it. Enough years passed that as I watched him read into his old age, his eyes went the other way, and by his mid-eighties he no longer needed glasses at all.

ALEC, BARBARA, URI, AND BETSY – 1940

We'd go to the beach with Barbara, or he'd take me to Innis Arden, the hilly, Greenwich golf club where he'd been a member since the 1940s. He had a little set of clubs made up for me and tried, mostly in vain, to cultivate some degree of interest in the game. It wasn't interest I lacked, but perhaps some actual degree of talent for the sport. I was impatient, at times likely unpleasant, and an overall golfing disappointment to him. Still, he never gave up, and got me another larger set when I was fourteen. "Ya canna knock the cover off the ball, boy." he used to say.

I just didn't get it. How could you hit it far if you didn't hit it hard? The subtlety of it all was lost on me. But he and I painted a picturesque image there at Innis Arden, the old Scot with his little blonde grandson. We'd have lunch with his friends and they'd discuss their games and their projects there at the club. He always made sure I was dressed appropriately, usually in shorts—which I hated—so that I looked like a proper young boy around the clubhouse.

Growing up, I never really understood the loss of Uri in the life of his parents. The scrapbooks are full of Alec and Uri skiing, swimming, and traveling together. He was of course the natural pride of Barbara's life as well. I was too young to have a feel for this in the early days, but now with the letters it's becoming more obvious. Mom and

I spent a lot of time in Greenwich, and even before Uri was lost I had begun to fill a spot in my grandfather's heart. Thirty-three years later, I would become Uri in his mind when we spent his last weeks in that same fifth-floor apartment.

Grandpa had just turned sixty, and I was four when he first appears in my memory. His apartment in Greenwich had a little balcony looking out to the east over the harbor. There was a small table there, and two chairs. We'd read or play cards, or I'd watch Grandpa tend his flower boxes. He was always snipping, and for some reason I liked the rubber ball with the little chrome showerhead that he watered with. He'd squeeze it to suck water out of the bucket, then go around to his four boxes, watering very evenly and slowly. He was never in a hurry, no matter what he did.

Routines were always a comfort to my grandfather, and so they are to me. I strive to keep my keys always in the designated place, and the same with my various pairs of glasses. I care which pocket holds my penknife, which the lip balm, and I always have a guitar pick in my watch pocket. I now know why Grandpa and Grandma always washed the dishes as they went. The morning's breakfast bowl, spoon and cereal box were always laid out the night before. Hardtack, English orange marmalade, and that view right out Greenwich Harbor—there was nothing to do but sit down to it.

I can remember when I wasn't able to reach any but the lowest button on the elevator. It was the "B" for basement. At the age of four it was my job to push that "B" button. I could take us somewhere, but without a boost could not get us back again. I was the master of getting us to the basement. That's where Grandpa kept his Cadillac. He got a new one every two years and said it was cheaper that way, but I think he just felt he deserved that nice, new, comfortable Caddy. He liked to be seen driving it. The garage was built for much smaller cars. All this time, parking successively longer and longer Cadillacs in that concrete space beneath the building. He sure had it down—perfect economy of motion. At eighty-nine he made use of every adjustable mirror. That stuffy, close-cut Scottish mustache would elevate up and to the left just an inch as he backed smartly around the huge concrete pillars and smoothly into his tiny parking space. The magnificent swell of fenders and fins was everywhere in that angled and ramped basement—and I was proud that my Grandpa drove a Cadillac.

It would be easy enough, and perfectly appropriate, to mix the twelve summers I spent in Greenwich. I'm not sure that I can separate them in my mind with any precision anyway. It represents a continuum now—yearly snapshots of a different life and small adventures away from home. When I was fourteen, Mom drove me to Union Station in Washington, DC and let me take the train alone to Greenwich for the first time. What a different world we lived in! I could ride all the way to New York City, switch trains at Grand Central and be in Greenwich an hour later without anyone being worried about me.

Those first summer visits come back in bits and pieces. The feeling is there—linked memories that keep spurting out. It starts with that old elevator. It was creaky, and as I later noted, paneled in maple veneer. There would be a time at sea a dozen years later on a cruise with Grandpa when the sounds of creaking veneer on an ocean liner would remind me of that elevator. The reinforced diamond-shaped window of the elevator, and the matching ones on the heavy doors at each floor, passed each other to give quick glimpses of identical corridors. And the singing cables. I liked to read the warning label, and when I was alone finally got up the nerve to hit the emergency stop button between floors. I would turn the lights off and see how high I could count—scaring myself about getting stuck in this dark silent space.

I noticed during Grandpa's last days in the late '70s that very little had changed in the apartment building since my childhood. Harbor Heights had that old English sterility—marble floors with big Turkish-looking brass urns filled with sand in the corners. You seldom met anyone in the halls or lobby. It was a six-story building divided in two by the lobby and an outdoor patio beyond. It was identical reversed twins of itself, mirror imaged. As long as I could remember, Mr. Abbott was usually there in the lobby wearing his grey Harbor Heights uniform with maroon piping. He was skin and bones, much older than Grandpa, and I was never sure what he did. He had a little broom and dustpan and sometimes swept up a little in the corners of the sparse, echoing lobby. Often he was asleep in his chair when we'd pass through.

As a little kid, when I came into the building it was possible to make a mistake. After turning into the left half, but then making a quick right into the little room where the mailboxes were, you could come out of the mail room and turn left instead of right. A few times I entered the opposite side and became confused. Later as an eight-year-old, I got up the nerve to explore the whole building. I would travel the elevator and stairwells of the mirror image, and it gave me the eeriest feeling. I never felt comfortable there. Somehow the left side, where we lived, was familiar, even on different floors. A couple of times I went to the fifth floor on the other side, where everything was backwards in every way. I imagined myself in a science fiction story or one of those horror comic books. Though I was tempted, I never had the nerve to ring the doorbell in the apartment that matched ours. It was way too scary then to think of who or what might open that door.

The apartment overlooked the old Greenwich High School and well kept playing fields immediately below and to the right. Straight ahead was the view right out Greenwich Harbor, and on a clear day we could see Island Beach in the distance. Alec, Barbara and I sometimes took the ferry there for a day of swimming and playing at the beach. More often though we'd go to Greenwich Point, which was closer, with less hustle and bustle. Grandpa always swam out far from shore, and breast-stroked from one flagpole on the beach to the next. They were one-quarter mile apart, and as I got older I would join him. He told me that if you alternated with the sidestroke you could swim all day long if you had to.

From our apartment window, the New Haven Line passed just in front of the harbor. Sometimes we'd take the train into New York City when Grandpa had business there. He took me to the top of the Empire State Building, which had an elevator that made my stomach drop, and we walked up the steps inside the Statue of Liberty.

It's hard to remember the transition between being four years old, tagging along on Grandpa's long walks, and later, when I used to explore the town on my own. The same cop directed traffic at Greenwich Avenue and West Elm for years. He knew the walking habits of all his citizens, and in the later years gave Grandpa all the time he needed.

Alec saw Greenwich grow from a small, perfectly run New England village, to a suburb, and soon a landing zone for all the office buildings that had begun to climb their way out of the city. Even as a child I felt uncomfortable about the city coming to Greenwich, and the crowds that began to fill the roads and the beaches. But Grandpa viewed all growth as business, and business was always good. The disappearing countryside and the multiplying freeways were all a sign of progress to him, and he never thought it an inconvenience to share his Greenwich with so many new people.

One day we were walking in Bruce Park. Grandma was taking her heart medicine in those days and couldn't go walking with us, but Alec and I would go for an hour or two most mornings. The Bruce Museum was a four-story nineteenth century Victorian mansion that had been dedicated to a surprisingly varied natural history collection. We'd go there almost every summer. The carved spiral staircases were lined with butterflies and insect collections—all pinned to the walls or arranged in replicate surroundings of a world they no longer inhabited. There were rooms displaying colonial dress uniforms, furniture and coats of armor. But my favorites were the reptile rooms, and the display cases full of dinosaur bones.

We passed one of the small lakes in the park near the fields where the various Greenwich teams play baseball in the evening—I must have been seven that year. I remember asking Grandpa if there were any fish in the lake. He replied that there might be a few little ones, three or four inches long, but nothing more. With that, a splashing and commotion began right in the middle of the lake, fifty feet from shore. Something big flipped and jumped, and all of a sudden this trail of leaping and splashing came right toward us. Whatever it was, it was hopping on top of the water, and here it came—flipped out of the water and landed at our feet. I picked up the fish, which Grandpa said was a carp, and it was a foot long. It stretched and flapped in my hand, and flopped loose on the shore before I could throw it back. We couldn't imagine what could have been chasing that fish, or why it chose just that moment to prove its existence to us with an apparent attempt at suicide.

Back at Harbor Heights, when I was eight or nine, the rooftop became my newfound escape. From there I surveyed the town and rolling hills to the northwest, as well as the arrowhead of Greenwich Harbor opening into the Sound. I could see the siren on a tower above the fire station that sounded every evening at 6 p.m. The roof was flat, with three-foot walls around the entire perimeter. There were drains everywhere, special rooms with big ventilator fans, plenty of smaller roof fans and vents, and little metal stairways that led over the brick walls from one graveled section of the roof to another. I spent hours up there over many summers and never saw another soul. I flew paper airplanes off the roof and dropped gravel and water balloons on selected targets six stories below. There were outdoor terraces with potted plants and more sand-filled urns, as well as tables and chairs that no one ever sat in. No one seemed to notice my bombing, but Mr. Abbott must have wondered where the ripped balloons and gravel were coming from.

By the time I was fourteen I had a new reason to hang out on the roof. I had begun a new hobby—smoking cigarettes. When I started, at eleven or twelve, my mom and stepfather Steve liked Cavaliers, which came in a sealed can of two hundred. When the tin was full, you pulled a little ribbon and up would pop a nice little stack. My friends and I could always cop a few without the folks getting wise. Later when they switched to Chesterfields, then Pall Malls, we'd steal them by the pack from the carton. It seems inconceivable to me now that we started so young, and also that Betsy and Steve were continually smoking in the car with all five kids and the windows rolled up. All the same, it seemed glorious to me at the time to head up to the roof in Greenwich and smoke my fool head off.

Uri

My research of the *Enterprise* logs and the squadron chronicle gives me access to information that Uri was unable to reveal. Before actually joining the ship on December 24th, the men of Torpedo 90 were doing their last-minute training around the islands of Kauai and Molokai. In both Hadley's chronicle and Uri's letters you can sense the building excitement. They practiced bombing targets on and around the islands, and spent time learning the systems and characteristics of their newly refurbished airplanes. Night carrier flights, then in their infancy, required outstanding instrument-flying proficiency. Airborne radar, also a new development, would guide you to your target. Your instruments would help you fly back to the ship. In a four-hour flight, you might not once see the horizon.

There was plenty for the new aircrews to get used to. Already in the few months before embarkation, accidents were occurring. The squadron was steeled to the task ahead by these early tragedies, but they felt finished with preparation. Everyone knew it was necessary, but it was all theoretical, an exercise, and they were done with it. As young men with the war right in front of them, there was apprehension, but they were even more impatient to begin. I can feel this determination creeping into Uri's letters.

*I remember that in one of your last letters
you said that people back home seem to think
that the war with Japan will be over pretty
soon. I don't know how they ever get that
idea — I wish it was true. It's a fact that
every place we attack we always win, and
expect to, and our losses are relatively light,
but relatively can cover a multitude of sins.
And the reason we will continue to win is
not that we are so much smarter or better
fighters or any such editorial page stuff,
but merely because we send in such an
overwhelming superiority of equipment each
time. But every time as we get nearer to Japan,
this superiority must get bigger and bigger,
and takes longer and longer to get together.
I'm not pessimistic either, but I have slowed
down in my thinking since 6 months ago. I
remember when the so-called German uprising
took place everyone thought the war with
them would be over in a few months. Even
Eisenhower predicted Sept. 15th. And look
at us now. The war here could last another
1½ - 2 years. I don't say it will, but it might.
However it might be sooner, and I wouldn't
be too surprised at attacking the Japanese
coast before this cruise is over.*

The *Enterprise* (CV-6) had just returned from Leyte Gulf, the largest
sea battle in naval history. The third week of October 1944 had found
her just west of the Philippines where US submarines made contact
with advance units of the Japanese fleet. The Allied fleet was about
to start the final push that would drive the enemy out of the Philippines. It appeared that the Japanese navy was entering the Sulu Sea
to confront the US invasion of the major island of Leyte, their central
stronghold. The enemy knew that after a string of defeats, their only
chance to win the war was to trap us at Leyte Gulf and destroy our
invasion fleet in one culminating battle.

A decoy force consisting of four ineffective Japanese carriers, and only a few qualified pilots, came down from the north. Simultaneously, the southern and central enemy battleship groups swarmed toward Leyte Gulf. Although heavily outnumbered and out-trained, the enemy had the advantage of hundreds of land-based bombers from the big island of Luzon to the north. Japanese odds also improved when the US Third Fleet, under Admiral "Bull" Halsey, fell for the ruse. With his carrier task force he steamed north to intercept the decoy carriers and left San Bernardino Strait, and therefore the Leyte Gulf invasion force, almost totally unprotected. Communications were misunderstood on both sides, but Halsey had taken the *Enterprise* and her task force out of the picture. His confusing and misleading orders had the potential of giving the naval advantage back to the Japanese.

Fortunately there were tactical errors on both sides, and Leyte Gulf played out in favor of the Allies. Pilots flying off US carriers had made the difference. Airpower from a mobile platform proved superior to the shipboard gun power that had dominated sea battles in the past. By late 1944, the Japanese had fewer airplanes than the Allies had surface vessels.

With the new battle cruise looming, it was time for the *Enterprise* to enter the arena once again. She was ready to take aboard the air group, re-name the task force, and change her final designation to CV(N)-6. It was about to be official, and it was secret. She would become the world's first all-weather, night-designated aircraft carrier, and she was on her way to the South China Sea. Her bombers now belonged to Torpedo 90, instead of Kippen's illustrious Torpedo 10, which had passed into *Enterprise* history.

The sea and sky were bright blue and beautiful on Christmas Eve, 1944, as the *Big E* prepared to sail out of Pearl Harbor. The first mix-up of the cruise made its departure later than expected. Both squadrons launched from their land base, expecting the ship to be underway, but were soon vectored back to Barbers Point while the carrier had an antenna changed out. It wasn't critical, but typical of the last-minute snafus that seemed endemic to military life.

You don't just crane sixty-three aircraft aboard a carrier while she's dockside. The ship has to be underway in open water, wind at the bow, so they can be landed on the flight deck. Both the fighters and bombers had to return, shut down, and be capped off with fuel while their aircrews climbed out of the cockpits with their gear and stood around on the tarmac, not knowing what had happened. In today's world, it is hard to imagine two complete squadrons being accidentally launched to an aircraft carrier that was not yet underway.

URI, BOTTOM RIGHT ABOVE THE WING

At 1600 (4 p.m.) they launched again, this time to complete their rendezvous. Both squadrons put on a show for the crowds they were leaving behind at Barbers Point, as well as another low-altitude display for the crew waiting aboard the *Enterprise*. As the aircraft arrived, the band played, and the ship's company lined the flight deck in their dress whites. The *Big E* finally began landing planes at 1700, and all were safely aboard as the sun faded into the sea.

The ship's guns were at the ready as they passed westward through the sub nets, and the new aircrews were struck by a realization. They were aboard the most celebrated aircraft carrier in the Pacific, with two superbly trained combat squadrons, VF(N)-90 and VT(N)-90, and for the first time, they were at war.

About 1600, the order came to man planes and we were off again, this time for good, to fly aboard the Enterprise which was to be our home, companion and true love for God only knew how long. It was a good sight to see the old girl sweeping majestically along over the unbelievably blue tropical sea and to many of us, who had sailed aboard her before, it was like coming home, in a sense at least. All of us felt the pride that a true sailor feels when he says "That's MY ship!" The two squadrons put on quite a show for the ship before she finally turned into the wind and prepared to take us aboard. The fighters landed first as usual, and, as usual, the first one took a wave-off! The spectators in the gun galleries and catwalks saw a big red Santa Claus painted on the engine cowl of the first fighter as he roared by—the only reminder that the Yuletide season was so close at hand. It took about an hour and a half to land the thirty-six fighters and twenty-seven torpedo planes but everyone got aboard without mix-up—some of us only took one pass!!

— from Hadley's VT(N)-90 squadron history

The F6F Hellcat was a smaller and faster plane than the TBM Avenger torpedo bombers flown by Uri's squadron. It was designed to outfight the Japanese Zero in air combat, which it was able to do primarily as a result of its firepower and heavier armor. The Zero had the edge in maneuverability, but just couldn't stand up to the six 50-caliber machine guns of the Hellcat and its higher speed at all altitudes. It was a rugged airplane, designed to keep flying if hit, and could escape an attacking Zero by initiating a full-on dive if necessary. It could also carry a substantial bomb load as well as the five-inch rockets carried by the TBMs. Best of all, it was easy to fly and inspired confidence in the large numbers of new pilots who were being trained to fly it. The young aviators were especially proud of their Hellcats, which would end up leading the skies with a nineteen-to-one kill-to-loss ratio. It was the Avengers, and their fighter escorts—the Hellcats—that would fly from the *Enterprise* deck for the remainder of the war.

*

It's getting harder to read these letters, and my wife can't handle it at all. I've just finished 1944, as Uri left Hawaii to join the *Big E*. Betsy's three older brothers are in the Army in Europe and she's living in Columbus with her parents, younger brother Ted, and of course me. Christmas is depressing in the Magnuson household—most of the family is in danger, and out of touch.

Uri isn't able to tell Betsy that he's about to join his ship, but she somehow knows it. He's still writing every day, but there's no more news about the squadron living in BOQ Dog, or descriptions of his days on the airbase. In fact there isn't much he can tell her now, except how much he worships her and yearns to be with her again when it's all over. He's more philosophical in these later letters, and sometimes comments on the war effort.

December 22, 1944

I get discouraged reading some of the war news these days. Dugout Doug MacArthur's dogfaces are as usual all bogged down in Leyte, Philippines, and I'll bet you they have to send Marines in again to help him out as they already have in 2 or 3 cases in the Pacific. That means longer and harder cruises for guys like me. And things aren't moving any too fast in Europe either. I'm sorry to say I think there's a lot of fighting ahead — although this white boy after he gets home from this cruise ain't going to do any of it — or any night flying either!

I've just begun to look at the letters from aboard the *Enterprise* and something about them is different than the earlier ones. They appear to be written in haste and with much larger script. The pages for the first time are numbered with big Roman numerals, and the lines sprawl unevenly. Few of the letters from late December and early January are in envelopes. I'm trying to get them in order, but they're pretty mixed up. Christmas Day's letter is sitting on top, but it looks like Uri wrote long letters over several days, then mailed them out in chunks.

Christmas was the first new day aboard ship and he's just getting moved in. The aircrews have been given a talk by the censors and now Uri has gone back to rewrite his letters of the last few days. He says that much of what he'd written earlier would have been cut out, so he just starts over. He tells Betsy that he won't likely be flying as much in the future because of his training duties—only the most important flights. But given that he flew regularly with the skipper, Uri knew that he would still be doing plenty of flying. Kippen was the most experienced combat pilot in the squadron and was likely to be on all the "important" flights. He led by example and wouldn't have had it any other way. Most importantly, the entire squadron feels inspired by Kip's leadership, and Uri is proud to be flying with him. Betsy may have taken some comfort in Uri's words, but she knew he flew with Kip, and had to be aware how hollow they felt.

There are twenty letters before me—most are six pages or longer and some are packed together, two or three at a time, in a single envelope.

Christmas Day 1944

This Christmas day is not much different from any other day except for a turkey dinner and some nice speeches from the higher ups aboard, including an admiral. This ship is a fine steady one, and although it rolls and pitches somewhat, it is a comfortable ship, and will be as long as no ones is dropping bombs on us, which I hope is never. I went to church today, and although it was not very impressive it was kind of nice to sing a few Christmas carols together..........

Merry Christmas again from me to you and Sandy. May God keep you both and bring us all back together again soon.

Love and kisses - Uri

*

Of course—singing! It's come up three or four times. Back in the BOQ Dog days there were sing-alongs with bands at the officers' club. I hadn't really thought of it until now. I've been a music nut, playing in bands since my late teens. Uri talks about listening to records and radio shows with Betsy, and I remember now that like myself, he sang in the choir in college. I get the feeling that Uri would have enjoyed playing music, too. I can tell from his letters that he had that way about him. There are continuing little threads—similarities between us—to follow here.

It was 1950, and as fourth graders my best friend Joe Stearns and I were sent to Avondale Country School, near Beltsville, Maryland. Avondale had about fifty students and went to the eighth grade. Joe and I attended just that one year, but it left an impression. Each grade had its own teacher, so it was, in effect, eight one-room schoolhouses. Our teacher, Mr. Jim O'Kane, looked like Clark Kent in khakis. He was funny, but tough, and somehow made us fourth-grade boys believe in things like poetry and art. It wasn't really much of a military school, though we had to shine our shoes, polish our brass buttons, and wear our ACS gray "fore and aft" caps. There wasn't much of a sports program, or even an athletic field as I remember. The number one school pastime between classes or after school was marbles. We'd scratch out our circles in the dirt and play every chance we got. We all had our marble collections with our aggies (agates), steelies (ball bearings), bunkers (big marbles) and others that we classified by type. Some types were considered more valuable, and the goal was to capture other people's best marbles in playground matches. You always had a special "shooter." I still have my marble collection and have been teaching my grandkids to play. I've even stashed away "Junior," my old, chipped-up blue and red double horseshoe shooter, to keep him from getting lost.

Joe and I were day students. We went home after school, but there were also boarders. One year my parents boarded me at school for two weeks in December and I remember only one thing about it, but it changed my life. We had a bugler, Bill Okus, who blew reveille, quarters, taps, and a few other calls throughout the day. He was our school bell. I used to like to listen to him practice. When my parents boarded me at the school, I scrounged up an old bugle, went into the vacant gym, and blew my brains out for two straight weeks.

The sound of the horn in that empty gym was magic to me, and I discovered that I could easily spend hours at a time practicing. I loved the look of the horn, the gleaming, spiraled construction, the way it felt in my hands. But mostly I was fascinated by the way I was starting to control that sound. I liked learning how to play it, and within a few months was able to position myself as the number one (and only) apprentice bugler at Avondale County School. I played the calls for two or three days that spring, as Bill Okus was plenty healthy and seemed never to miss a day. But that didn't matter to me. What I learned was that I loved to sit by myself with that bugle for hours on end. This trait, still a big part of my makeup, led me eventually to become a musician.

By the seventh grade I had switched to piano. Even as a little kid I could pick out melodies by ear, so the following year Mom found me a teacher. Mary Izant Couch was in her eighties, and I know that I never made much of an impression on her. She was an old school Russian concert pianist, trying to make me understand the world of classical music. I was an eighth-grade kid who spent much of my time in the woods, riding my pony Blackie, or shooting things with my pellet rifle. I showed up one day for a lesson with worms in my pocket, and I had the audacity to argue with her about music. Once a week after school I would walk to her house. She'd immediately take me to the bathroom to wash my hands. This was something I evidently couldn't do well enough myself. She would scrub them with industrial soap and a fingernail brush. She would pull all my fingers apart and force her thumb back and forth hard into the webbing between my fingers until they were raw. "You must stretch ze skeen between ze fingers every day," she would tell me, "and you cannot touch my ivories unless your hahnnds are perfect."

At my first piano recital I played, quite poorly, Beethoven's Sonata in C. Then I announced to the audience that I would now play it the way that I thought that it should be played. I ripped sloppily through the piece at twice the proper tempo, and Mrs. Couch never forgave me. But even today, at the age of sixty-eight, I still do the thumb-finger pressure stretch every day before my practice.

I can't help but wonder whether there would have been a musical relationship between my father and me. So much seems a matter of chance. In fact, the bugle experience seems the most significant, if only because I learned at that time the joys (and rewards) of solitary practice. I get a general feeling from the letters that I have read so far that Uri also valued the time he spent alone, and that he spent a lot of it listening to music.

*

When I've found everything I can from Uri, I'll be left with what I've been afraid to look at—twenty-six unopened letters from Betsy that evidently reached the ship too late for him to read. They've been sealed since she wrote them and I have no idea what to expect. Really, there should be no difference. It's just that I'll be opening them instead of Uri. It's almost as if I'm intercepting my father's mail, even though it's sixty-five years later.

The very physical act of opening them carries another emotional load for me. No one has seen the letters since she wrote them and she obviously never had the desire to go back and look at them herself. Why would she? She had written them without knowing, and it could only rekindle the pain to read them later. There is also a small stack of condolences written to her by Uri's squadron-mates that I will get to, perhaps last of all.

It's almost the New Year, and Uri's mood seems good. He's working hard and writing regularly. The format is a little woolier, as mentioned before, but the letters carry the common refrain. He loves her, worships her, and wants to get back to her as soon as possible. I can tell he's conscientious about his job. He's proud of his work and his squadron, and there is a rising pitch of excitement about the days and nights ahead.

December 30, 1944

Last night I had to stand a watch from 7 at night until 12:00. It was quite interesting to patrol the deck and look around all over. It was a beautiful night with a full moon, and you could see everything around very well. I could see everything but you darling, and you were there in my heart and in my imagination. There was a movie going on on the hangar deck, and I got a glimpse of it now and then. Alice Faye was in it. She is very much your type in face and figure, altho bigger all around, but I could just visualize you through her, because even her hair was done like yours. And when she grabbed ahold of Ameche, or whoever it was, it was quite a sight, believe me. Oh for the simple (?) pleasures of home.

I am enclosing a clipping out of the letter I transferred this from, showing you

how well I draw - together with some very
pertinent comments on how much I love you.

As always - Uri

By the way or draw a little how you look dinner. Of here, and at Well so loves you more on earth. And else could you so well, every bit of you are all mine.

you see, and one showing you bringing me cocktails before course you are fully dressed home I don't know long darling. I'm the guy that than any one or anything else I love you more than anyone love you, because I know every thought of yours and every bit of you are all mine.

Your Uri

It's New Year's Day now and all is well on Uri's "little Pacific cruise." There are athletics each day aboard ship. On the flight deck at midday they organize calisthenics and touch football when flight operations allow. Below, on the hangar deck, there are volleyball and basketball games. Uri calls it "the most comfortable way to fight a war that there is I guess—except for those hours you do the job you were brought for."

In this same letter Uri addresses a topic that needs to be conveyed in full ...

January 1, 1945

By the way, not to introduce too serious
a note, but I wanted to point out one thing
about when a person is reported "missing" and
was on a training flight, or far from combat
areas, where every rescue facility is available,
he is a gone goose for sure, but that does
not hold true in combat areas, where a guy
can come down, be picked up by some small
ship, and not even be reported for a long time,
or land on an island and live there until picked
up by air rescue facilities. A lot of those

guys are eventually found and picked up. I do not intend to be in any such unwelcome situation however. On re-reading this letter darling I want to emphasize again that the only reason I even brought up that "missing" business is because I remembered talking to you once and explaining how they even carried "missing" on the books when a guy was lost off San Diego or someplace, and I wanted to point out the difference. Last cruise a guy was missing, picked up by an Australian boat, shipped home on a slow tanker by mistake, & got home before his own ship did!

This commentary turns out to be prophetic. For two years after the battle in which he was lost, Uri was declared missing. My mother was in a state of limbo, praying that he would someday come walking back through the door. When she married Bob Stephens (Steve) in 1948, she still wasn't sure. Even late in her life she kept having that irrational feeling, but by this time it would come to her as a dream. There is more from his New Year's Day letter ...

I don't do a great deal of flying any more – and when I do it is with the skipper (Lt. Kippen) whom you probably remember from San Diego. He is a wonderful pilot with a great deal of experience, and being with him is quite comfortable, or at least as comfortable as those little things can be! However after this little cruise is over I know I will quit flying. I'm too old for that sort of stuff continually, and have too gorgeous a big blonde gal at home to cuddle up with to spend the next few years out on the deep Pacific. Just thinking of a cuddling session makes my poor old heart beat like a cheap alarm clock.

*

I can relate to Uri's sense of wonder at being out on the flight deck alone under the full moon. I spent my sophomore summer aboard a destroyer and we stood regular four-hour lookout watches. It's the

58

middle of the night. You're decked out in foul weather gear, outboard of the bridge, in your little metal yardarm lookout perch. The ship is slicing through huge troughs, waves are flying through the air, you're hanging on to the rail for dear life—somehow, it's great. It's the same feeling you get on the peak of a mountain you've just climbed. You're alive and you're on the edge. I've felt that same exhilaration flying high, dodging the clouds on the way back to the ship.

Each flying crewman had been adding to his personal survival gear:

Ever since we left Pearl Harbor we have been gradually accumulating more and more equipment until now, when we struggle out to the planes, we are fully prepared to set up light housekeeping under any given set of conditions for any length of time. Our gear includes a hunting knife, a thirty-eight calibre revolver, one and two cell flashlights, a pencil flashlight, waterproof charts, flags, whistles, heavy Marine shoes, vitamin capsules, first aid kit, Mae West life jacket, parachute harness, chart board, helmet and goggles, flight suit, Very pistol and flares, dye marker, and a back pack which contains "K" rations, machete, malted milk tablets, jack knife, whet stone, mosquito net hood, poncho, water, first aid kit, fishing tackle, more flares, smoke bombs, twine, matches, compass, gloves, and various other useful items. Each man also has a one-man raft secured to his parachute pack.

— from Hadley's VT(N)-90 squadron history

Remember that all of this gear had to be attached to your harness for each flight, then lugged up from below decks and across the flight deck. This was the minimal stuff you wanted with you if you departed company with your aircraft. Just keeping track of it all and deciding how to organize it safely in the cockpit was a matter of continual experimentation. Everyone had their own plan, which led to endless discussions back aboard the ship. What needed to be accessed first? Was it the first aid kit, or maybe the revolver? Surely nothing could interfere with the Mae West inflatable life jacket, but what about the smoke flares? If you went into the drink, the first priority was being picked up—and fast. If you aren't found right away your chances of being rescued at all diminish drastically. It's so hard to see someone in the waves. I learned in my helicopter-flying days that it was a big ocean out there. We spent many days, hours at a stretch, searching the windswept waves for accident survivors or a man overboard. Your eyes start to play tricks on you. You think you see things that aren't there, and you just know that you are missing things that *are* there.

*

The *Big E* is gearing up for the full-on invasion of Luzon, and the pre-invasion bombing of Formosa (now Taiwan). Luzon is the most strategically important island in the Philippines. The *Enterprise* once again joins Task Force 38, now under the command of Vice Admiral John S. McCain, Sr. Six carriers are joined by another six light-carriers, and combined with three battleships, numerous cruisers, light cruisers, and destroyers. This formidable armada is the primary attack wing of the US Navy Third Fleet in the Pacific, and still commanded by Admiral "Bull" Halsey. The only night flights so far from the deck of the *Big E* are submarine patrols (ASPs). No enemy ships have yet been sighted. MacArthur and the amphibious forces will land at the northern end of the valley that leads to Manilla, tracing the same steps the Japanese had taken four years earlier. The task force is there to protect the landing force from any reinforcements from the remaining Japanese fleet, and to attack day and night targets as identified within the invasion plan.

> *Another briefing lecture this afternoon dealt with the geography of Luzon and Formosa and the Nansei Shoto. They also gave us the word on survival. Very interesting dope but we hope we never have the occasion to put it to use. Formosa especially sounds a little rugged—the natives there hate the Japs but they also hate Americans and some parts of the island are reported to be inhabited by the old fashioned type of head hunters. One would undoubtedly have an exciting time of it if forced down there.*
> — from Hadley's VT(N)-90 squadron history

One can't help but wonder: What are the new type of headhunters? You have to admire Hadley's offbeat sense of humor. Uri feels drained from all the lectures and meetings. Maps need to be studied and understood. There are continuing survival presentations in the event one finds himself without his airplane.

January 4, 1945

I had to laugh in your letter where you said you wished something would happen in the Pacific War so that it would move along faster! Well I can assure you that whatever happens in that war, your darling husband will be very much in on it for the rest of this cruise.

In one of the letters I read today, he alludes to Betsy's "starting things" romantically. She's teasing him about it and he's kidding back about how that doesn't seem to be the problem—that she seems pretty much the instigator. Lots of flirtation on both sides with mutual threats of what they will do to each other when the cruise comes to an end. Here he speaks directly to me ...

Kiss and hug little Sandy for me, and Sandy you put your little arms around Mommy's pretty neck and give her a big hug and tell her time is flying, and Daddy will soon be back at her side.

No newsy items to report, but the sense of anticipation is building. The entire ship felt that something big was in the air. All four task groups of Task Force 38 have formed up and are heading north. Halsey had his four-star flag aboard the *New Jersey*, a fast battleship, while "Slew" McCain, with his three stars, commanded from the *Lexington*. Coincidently, my first carrier landings in 1965 were aboard the *Lexington*, which for years was stationed in Pensacola as a training ship for new naval aviators.

Friday, 5 January 1945

This is the date set for our meeting with the rest of the fleet. When we came up on deck this morning after chow, we beheld one of the most awe-inspiring sights that Navy men can ever see. Warships of every type and description lay halfway round the clock and as we steamed steadily toward them, more and more rose into sight over the horizon. We were witnessing one of the greatest accumulations of Naval strength ever seen in the Pacific. A few hours later ships were visible on all sides as far as the eye could reach. What a sight!! The surprising number of carriers of all classes, with complete screens, gave us some indication of the tremendous striking force as well as defensive power of our fleet.

— from Hadley's VT(N)-90 squadron history

In early January the first large-scale kamikaze attacks began in much of the Pacific Theater, but up to this time the *Enterprise* has been spared. She has been targeted, but so far the fighters and the outlying smaller ships of the task force have kept incoming planes at bay.

January 6, 1945

Things are sort of stalemated around here now, if you can call it that. I'm getting used to sleeping when I can, and with most of my clothes on. It's a pretty good habit to get into because you never know when you are going to have to move pretty fast. Most of your time is spent in the "ready room" which as you probably know from the movies, has comfortable cushioned leather seats, with a fancy board device which makes a desk out of it. The room is air-conditioned and very comfortable. It also has two-high let down bunks along the sides, where you can catch a nap while standing by for something to happen.

Uri strongly suggests that Betsy see the film "Fighting Lady" which he says is very realistic…

The photographer who took a lot of the action pictures is here now, altho the story wasn't mainly about this ship. He took our pictures running out to the planes the other day. (We ran right back because we didn't have anyplace to go!) So maybe I'll be a movie star if some talent scout sees me…

January 7, 1945

There was a story spreading around that someone heard "Tokyo Rose" broadcasting yesterday that there were fifteen "Kamikashi" pilots who had dedicated their lives to sinking this ship, because it had been a thorn in their side for so long. Probably good old *scuttlebutt like most of the stuff that spreads around here....*

Goodnight darling from your husband, who loves you and worships you, and dreams of you day and night.

Uri

ARMING A TBM AVENGER WITH THE MARK 13 TORPEDO

He then talks about his frustration with not having enough time to read. He's having to subsist on magazine articles when he has a chance. He's hoping they get a slow spell so he can get some regular sleep. He's more confident and committed as the *Enterprise* gets closer to the action, but signs this letter a little ominously ...

Oh well, it's a great life, wasn't it.

*

Uri seems to have hit his stride in explaining his daily life to Betsy. Reading his letters stirs up a familiar feeling that came over me during the earlier days of the Vietnam War. I'd been assigned to a squadron flying helicopters off the *USS Wasp* in the Atlantic, while many of my classmates and fellow pilots from Annapolis were flying combat missions in Southeast Asia. I was dedicated to the service and can remember being possessed by the desire to prove myself in battle. People used to say that it was the duty of every generation to go to war—a patriotic rite of passage. I volunteered for duty in Light-Attack Helicopter Squadron Three. They were flying the new Huey Cobras in Vietnam. The Cobra was the most badass-looking chopper ever. The fuselage was only three feet wide, and it bristled with rockets and guns. I could just see myself diving into the enemy and shooting up a storm. It was like the cover of a World War II comic book in my head—people scrambling, explosions all around them, the sky filled with helicopters, rockets and smoke.

Mary Lynn and I had been married for almost three years when I told her I'd decided to volunteer for HAL-3. She was quiet, but that evening after dinner she said, "You really do want to follow in your father's footsteps, don't you?" She was crying, and her meaning was clear. Our son was three years old, his name was Sandy. How else could it go?

That conversation began an internal dialogue that led a few months later to my decision to leave the naval service. I had begun to play music in coffee houses and meet people who felt differently about our involvement in Vietnam. At the same time I was hearing the stories from my fellow flight instructors in Pensacola. Many of them were Marines and had just returned from Vietnam. Some of them were burnt and scarred, and many were filled with an intense anger that would erupt as soon as the subject came up. More than once I heard the now well-known expression, "Kill 'em all and let God sort 'em out later." It was a sick joke, but some meant it. We know that war dehumanizes. It changes those who have seen too much, and it affects everyone from that time forward. All the more important that we're called upon as an absolute last resort. Going to war must be the very last option so that families are not devastated by needless or misguided policy.

I started to have second thoughts. For our country to have risen to the challenge of Germany and Japan in my father's day was as noble a cause as can be found. The threat was clear and we became involved, barely in time, for all the right reasons. But does this mean that every generation should have a war to fight, and that all young men should aspire to such a thing? Won't there be a day when we've gotten past this?

My four-year required commitment was extended a year-and-a-half because of the war, but I was eligible for release in six more months and took that option. It turns out to have been a good choice. Many HAL-3 pilots were shot down. The Cobra, although deadly fearsome head on, had minimal fire suppression to the rear once it passed the target. The enemy learned that once you went by, he could jump up from his hole in the ground and shoot you down from behind. That chopper may have looked like the nastiest war machine of all time, but it was vulnerable. Soon I had friends from my old shipboard helicopter squadron in POW camps—and they were the survivors.

*

The first ten days at sea quickly brought the *Enterprise* back into the combat theater. The fighter pilots of VF(N)-90 were getting some action but the shipboard excitement was not spilling over to Uri's squadron, who had not yet flown their first combat mission. The Hellcats were beating the bomber boys to the punch, and the TBM pilots and crews were anxious to get into it. The day fliers were smashing up enemy warehouses and supply routes, and hopefully soon it would be the job of the after-dark team to keep the Japanese from rebuilding at night.

As I reread the accounts in Hadley's journal for the fourth or fifth time, I'm just starting to get the timeline in my head. I still haven't read any of Uri's letters mailed that first week of January 1945, but they're piled in front of me now. It's evident that the war is heating up again. Years ago when I did some research on the *Big E*, I hadn't yet discovered Hadley's squadron history, and it was only there that I could learn which missions had included my father.

January 8, 1945

I'm sorry to hear Bill Lindeman died from his injuries. He seemed a fine kid, and representative of the best we have in this country. We here have our troubles along that line too, but the custom is to forget it and not even refer to it, even if you were just

*playing rummy with the guy 6 or 7 hours ago.
It may seem callous, but it is the only way
to do, from any practical point of view. Some
day there will be a period of mourning for
all that have gone, but until that time we all
have to pull together and do our best to end
things as quickly as possible.*

(and later in the same letter)

*Your letter sure is sweet honey. However
you should stop using that marihuana. I mean
of course when you said I was good looking!
I know absence is supposed to make the
heart grow fonder, but it still can't make a
silk purse out of a sow's ear (namely - me).*

*Well goodnight love, sleep tight, daddy will
be home one of these days and you won't get
a chance to sleep that much. I love you old
darling, so very much.*

Your, Uri

I thought that the reference to marijuana was amusing in that it was written in 1945, and I was surprised to hear my father speak of it so offhandedly. I didn't think it was yet in the national consciousness. Evidently it was already in use, if only by jazz musicians.

Of course by the late '60s, many of us had inhaled, myself included. Some of the junior officers in my squadron got together and gave it a try one evening. Someone had procured some hashish from an enlisted man on base. We really didn't understand how to smoke it, and none of us felt that we had gotten high. It turned out that getting caught smoking pot in the Navy at that time would have meant a dishonorable discharge. We only tried it once. Our skipper heard rumors and put out the word on the sly that it better not ever happen again. I remember thinking at the time that this was a wise leadership move. There was no fuss, but everyone got the message.

January 11, 1945

Dearest Betsy,

I missed writing last night because I was awfully busy, and times kept getting pretty well mixed up. We are supposedly on a complete night schedule now, with breakfast at 2:30 in the afternoon and dinner at 12:00 at night, but actually it doesn't work out so smoothly and you find yourself just getting sleep in odd doses. Things were pretty interesting for me, and will be again early tomorrow I expect. I hope pretty soon we get a rest of some kind.....

... There isn't much news I can write you darling. I would suggest this, that knowing in a rough sort of way what we do, you keep all your newspaper clippings of things that are happening in this general area, and then compare them with the dates of my letters, and altho you will never know where I am, later on you could always give a good guess as to where I have been...

... Things are quite tense here now, something like sitting on the edge of a volcano that you do not know when it is going off. However if you sat on that same volcano long enough and nothing happened, you would take that sort of life as a matter of course and cease to worry about it, and that is the stage we are in now.

I'm glad to hear Sandy is behaving so well and looking so good. I hope he turns out to be a good boy, and I'm sure he will with a mother that takes such good care of him all the time, and is so good herself. Gosh knows his old man hasn't done much in his bringing up!

Betsy

I have been avoiding reading the last batch of twenty-six letters from Mom until now. They are unopened and that alone is foreboding. Most of them are sure to be from that period when she was writing but getting no response, and I'm not anxious to confront them. They would have reached him in January at some point, but mail deliveries were sporadic during this active combat period. Mail was flown to the carriers when possible, but the task force was on the move and it's obvious that Uri had seen no mail for several weeks. I have only read a few of my mother's letters up until now, and none since he's joined the *Enterprise*.

I have the pile of yellowed, fragile envelopes in front of me. They are all unopened and have a big, black "X" crayoned over Uri's Fleet Post Office address. There is a magenta rectangular stamp with the words *Returned to Sender* and *Unclaimed*, and the outline of a hand pointing sternly to the left. The first is from January 2, 1945, and they stop a few weeks after Uri was lost. They're mostly big fat letters and I've got a shaky reluctance about opening them at all. She can't know, because she's still writing to him, but she's got to be worried that she isn't getting any mail in return.

*

It's still hard for me to believe that she never told me about any of this. Mom wasn't one to keep secrets. She was famous for her stories around the dinner table and couldn't resist telling all. But apparently this was too close to home. She married for the third time in 1997 to a Canadian who had settled in the Smokies twenty years before. Ted Williams had been a plant manager for Boeing in Seattle, and a semi-pro hockey player in his younger days. He had only a third-grade education, and hilariously created entirely new words throughout his conversation. But he was a skilled builder and you had the feeling he could build you a skyscraper.

After Mom died in 2007, Ted found the letters in a box that he was about to throw away. He read one, felt the tears coming, boxed them up and sent them to me. He said that they weren't meant for him to read, but wanted me to have them. In truth, they weren't meant for me to read either, but I'm glad he put them in the mail. I'm not sure it would have been better for me to have received them earlier in my life. The perspective of the collapsed time behind us is more complete now. Life might seem long when it's all out in front of you, but now in our sixties we keep getting reminded of how fast it all goes by. An event that we thought occurred five years ago turns out to have been nine or ten, and we attend too many memorial services. In any case, we never could have gone through those letters while Mom was still alive. It wasn't something she could have talked about.

*

Just to slit the edge of the first letter, knowing that it has been sealed for sixty-five years, doesn't sit well. My stomach is churning and my body thermostat is out of kilter. Maybe I'm coming down with something and this is setting it off, but there's no avoiding it at this point. My much-diminished sense of smell still works well enough to place me with her as I open the first envelope. I put it to my nose and breathe deeply as I pull out the folded sheets. I expect to get the old attic smell, but could instead be imagining the barest whiff of perfume. I will repeat this with each of the next twenty-five letters.

Uri's been aboard the *Enterprise* for a week now but hasn't yet flown his first combat mission. Betsy knows he has left Hawaii, but that's about all. She's worried about him of course, but her attitude is positive. She's going to do what she needs to do.

December 31, 1944

It's New Years Eve darling. I just bathed and put a night gown on. I brushed my hair back, put fresh lipstick on and here I am in bed. I feel as if you are right here with me and I'm all fired up for you. I can recall so many times that I did this when we were physically together. I love you in so many ways, but nothing compares with the way that I feel when I know you are coming to me to take me in your arms and love me.

I don't know if I want to write about this or not. She describes each of their New Year's Eves together and goes into considerable detail. Now I'm faced with the problem of just how much to quote and how much to leave as a privileged secret between my mother and me.

Why did she keep the letters all this time? I can only wonder if she meant for them to come to me after she was gone. It's not that they are too specifically descriptive, if I can say it that way, but they are still the most personal of things. If either of them were still around I couldn't possibly be doing this. I don't want to be in violation of their privacy, but the way it all happened makes me feel that their story should be told. It's as if permission has been given.

The New Year's Eve letter is beautiful, and I'll let you read some more of it ...

I'll close now darling. I'm going to turn the lights out and listen to a special musical program that's just starting. I'm going to lie her and day dream of the dearest, sweetest, most lovable man in the world, and that's you. At twelve I'm going to talk to you for a while and I know you will hear

me. I know that you are thinking of
me and that especially at the time you
celebrate New Years Eve your love and
thoughts will come to me. I love you
very very much Uri. You're all I have
in many ways so be careful and hurry
to return to me.

>   Goodnight my angel,
>   your loving wife,
>   Betsy

It's not that their lives are unique. They're not extraordinary in
any way. All over the world, wives wait, children miss their fathers,
and the war goes on. And yet each story is important, each tragedy is
shared, and everyone is affected from that time forward. I'm trying to
learn about this and convey it while I have the chance. It's a way that
I can redeem the gift that I have been given. It's a story that is being
returned to its rightful owners—the living—those of us who shared in
the sacrifice.

Betsy and Uri had three New Year's Eves together. I should quote
the entire letter, but I know you get the idea. It's a twenty-three-year-
old girl talking, and she's not afraid to express her longings.

In the midst of all this, two of the Magnuson boys, Art and
Bill, will soon be coming home from Germany. The household is in
a tizzy, the rest of the family is excited, and Betsy feels isolated. She's
in a completely different mindset, and has just written her letter of
January 2nd …

I was so surprised and happy to hear
from you today. The letter is dated Dec
23rd and I know that you are on your
way. I know that you can write little,
if no news, but that doesn't matter when
you write the super love letters that you
do. This last letter is wonderful. I've
read it many times already and probably

will read it many more times before I go to sleep tonight.

All of the letters are romantic. Sometimes there's no news at all. I found my kindergarten class photo in this one and I'm shocked that I recognize my little girlfriend, Patsy Belt. I'm the smallest boy, and she looks startled, directly below me in the picture. My first experience of absolute emotional mortification occurred when Patsy introduced me to her mother by saying, "This is Sandy, the boy who kissed me." I turned beet-red and flashed on Patsy and me chasing each other around the dining room table in her house, and—oh my God—I must have kissed her. I think that event made me fear the ladies for years to come, and it quickly put an end to my first romance. Even now, looking at the photograph, I can remember Patsy and one other classmate's name from 1945.

SANDY: FOURTH FROM LEFT, MIDDLE ROW

January 3rd

In this letter there are more newsy items. She talks about finances, shopping for bras and panties, and winter gloves for me. She's just gotten a letter from Uri dated December 23rd, one day before embarkation. She can tell that he's on his way, and lets him know that she's waiting. She kids about me getting older and invading their "living room privacy," and says that they just may have to leave me out there and go to bed themselves, which "isn't too bad."

It's been snowing every day and she's taking me out on the sled. I'm evidently excited about school and she's going to get me new galoshes. My old ones are ripped and too small anyway.

January 5th

This one unabashedly smells of perfume. A little folded up note fell out of the letter when I opened it …

> I love you Uri. Always remember that
> you are all mine and always will be.

She's received four letters now since he's been aboard but she's trying not to expect mail. It's too easy to be disappointed.

> January 7, 1945
>
> I wish I knew more about what you
> are on, what group etc. As it is now I
> scan the newspapers every day looking
> for any mention of the boys I've met
> who are with you. There's a lot going on
> out there now and I constantly wonder
> what part you are playing in it. Do you
> fly much? Even tho it's of a different
> nature now I hope that your flying
> hours are much less now.

I knew these would be the most emotional letters to read. Uri and I were her world. I was hoping to take good enough notes that I wouldn't have to read them again, but I can see that it will not be the case. She asks about his flying and admits that she feels "damn shaky at times." About time passing, she writes: "It's like when you finally decide to do something and take the first steps, the thing seems almost accomplished."

My grandmother Clara sees the war as having at least two more years to go, while her husband Arthur thinks it will end almost any day. Betsy feels more like her mom, and her dad's predictions drive both of the women batty. She goes out to dinner, drinks with her friends and "gets a little tipsy."

Hurry up darling and come home so that you can be loved as you should be.

January 7th

For some reason, this letter has already been opened. Has a nice photo of Mom and me. She talks about how short I am. Says I'm smart as the dickens and use words like *perhaps, suppose, especially*. I always bring Uri into the conversation. When I meet people I always tell them right away that my dad is on an aircraft carrier fighting the Japs. She also writes that my grandmother Clara is a worrier and has a hard time eating. "I can't eat this food thinking about those poor boys going without. We don't have any right to laugh and party around when there is so much sadness." Even so, Betsy tells her that she does plenty of partying and when confronted, Grandma says, "Maybe I do, but I don't enjoy it."

January 8th

In this letter Betsy includes a cute photo of me laughing by the Christmas tree. We spent all day with her friend Bertie and her little boy, Wally, who is my age. The two women met each other at the hobby horse shop and began spending time with each other shortly thereafter. Bertie's husband Bob is missing in action, and she hasn't heard anything at all since the initial telegram a few weeks ago. She is being brave and hopes that he has been taken prisoner. Betsy and Bertie take us out for an ice cream cone while they buy their weekly carton of cigarettes. It's strange to read these specific events and have no memory of them whatsoever. I can't picture or remember Bertie or Wally in the least, but I do remember certain things. It must have something to do with the intensity of the experience. For example I do have a specific memory of posing with my mother for the painting, and I can remember her younger brother Ted playing tricks on me at the house in Columbus. He'd send me to the basement to look up the clothes chute, where he told me that I would see a clown. Then he'd pour a bucket of water down the chute. I remember sitting in that pile of wet laundry, bawling my eyes out.

Betsy relates the first time Uri turned off the lights and climbed into the bathtub with her. She tells him that they have to make sure to get a big tub when they have a house again. She likes to stay in her room at home with her letters and pictures and listen to the radio. From the photos, and maybe from my memory, I can just see her there.

This has to be done in small doses. So much needs to be digested. Meeting my mother in her early twenties is surprising. She's really just marking time until her man gets back, but I can tell she's getting more serious and organized. She's making plans and working toward his two-weeks "home leave" after the battle cruise ends, hopefully in June.

*

I know that she was never a complainer. If she was sick, you'd never know it. At eighty-five, when she started to get out of breath and needed oxygen, she still didn't complain at all, except for the part about having to "wheel around this damn bottle." She said, "All I know is that every time one of my friends gets on oxygen, next thing you know, they kick the bucket." It was always "kick the bucket" with Mom. She never seemed to worry about dying herself. When someone close to us died you could count on her to remind the whole family that "life is for the living." On its surface it seemed almost banal, but she would get our attention at dinner, and deliver her toast. I can see that for her, there was a deeper meaning in those words. It was a big part of how, twice in her life, she taught herself to go on.

I knew my mom for sixty-five years, and of course her later life comes in most clearly, then her middle age and her long married life with Steve. We lost Steve too early from heart disease and I wasn't around for much of her reaction to his death. I was in my late forties at the time, raising our family in Colorado. We were keeping in touch by telephone and she seemed to be handling it well. My youngest brother, Joe, said that it was tougher on her than she was letting on. She respected Steve's wishes—no memorial service, but a big party in his honor a year later.

We did the same for her when the time came. Joe and Ted put out the word and her mountain friends from all over dropped by the house to visit and talk about her. The barbecue was tended all day by the family, and the bar was well stocked. She would have enjoyed it. Everyone knew her, perhaps most of all as a storyteller, and many were told that day.

*

January 9th

They've only been separated four months and she's hoping to see Uri before her 24th birthday. She goes to see the movie "Mrs. Parkington" with her friend Burch. She talks about the war and a bet she made with Clara that it wouldn't end for two more years.

I've always hated the idea of growing older but I'd gladly skip the next five years or more if that would find us together living a normal life. The way things look now passing five years would come very close to arriving at the same time as the complete ending of this war. The Japanese are claiming all sorts of things such as large convoys heading toward Luzon, etc. but so far there has been no confirmation from our side, no doubt something big is on and we shall know soon. The European end of it doesn't look any too good, we've sure fooled ourselves over that part of it. No one thought they could last this long and here we are having setbacks.

Remember the saying Uri, "Only the good die young" – you rascal! Wait until you're in my arms again, you'll be sorry.

your loving wife,
Betsy

I keep remembering that Uri never did see these letters, though I'm sure Betsy sealed them up and mailed them right away. The postmarked date is usually just a day or two later than the date on the letter inside. This is my third time through the first dozen.

Going back and forth in time can be confusing. The letters don't match up in time because of the delay in mail deliveries, often as much as two or three weeks. Perhaps I should be mixing Uri's and Betsy's letters together chronologically instead of following each of my parents through similar periods of time. But, never mind. Nothing to do but plow on through them again—up until everything changes.

January 11th

There are two more pictures—one of me and one of Mom. It's been over two weeks since she's heard from Uri, and she's apprehensive. She thinks that he must be in on the Luzon invasion. She describes her loneliness for him and spends a page and a half describing her feelings when she thinks of him, "which is all the time." I'm trying to get used to my mother speaking of her strong desires, but again—I have to remember that she's just twenty-three. She never goes too far, saying that it would "put me in a bad way." She talks of their last time together ...

> I'll never forget as long as I live that parting in L.A. I can picture you exactly as you looked then anytime I want to, which is plenty often. I'm not a good one for flattery and description and the only way I can describe how you looked then is to say that you looked exactly like I would want the man who I loved with all my heart to look. Hurry up and come home will you so I can look some more.

She describes me and my sense of humor and says that my kindergarten teacher says I'm the smartest child she's ever had in her class. Betsy wonders if she tells all the mothers that. I can tell she thinks I'm smart too, but she's concerned about my height. Like many kids in those days I grew up in a cloud of second-hand cigarette smoke which might have something to do with it. I was battling genetics anyway. Uri was five-foot-seven, an inch shorter than his father Alec. I'm another inch down from Uri, but my son, at a whopping five-eight, is bringing us back up again.

January 13th

She's packed for both of us and we're getting ready to take the train to Greenwich. She still hasn't received any letters that Uri wrote after December 24th, and writes that she is anxious to hear about his Christmas and New Year's. She's looking at this trip, and being with Alec and Barbara, as another goal to accomplish. She says that dividing her time up into goals and accomplishments seems to make the time go faster. She plans to drop this letter in the mail at Grand Central Station in New York.

January 15th

We arrived in Greenwich on Sunday morning. It was cold on the train and no one got much sleep. Now we're at the apartment and have been talking almost continually since Sunday morning. Some of this is really fun to read ...

> Mother, Dad and myself haven't stopped talking since Sunday morning to say nothing of the chatter that Sandy has handed out. Honest to Pete Uri, he never stops, the folks are amazed at his line of talk, he has something to say on every subject. Mother said that I should be sure to tell you that her stomach has ached at Sandy since the minute he came in the door. There sure are crazy about him, and he has taken to them already. There's a lovely snow on the ground here and Sandy loves to play in it. Dad took him out Sunday, and he was out twice today, his cheeks turn rosy and he looks so healthy.

Most of my friends would probably agree with my mother's assessment—that I still have something to say on almost every subject. She talks about plans and what they will do when Uri finishes his cruise and is able to come home on leave. Alec and Barbara will keep me so that the two of them will have a chance to go somewhere. She chides him a little about not responding to her questions about this vacation and says that all he probably cares about is a "nasty four-letter word" which she admits that her plans include too, "and how !!!!!"

Betsy is getting better about looking ahead and not just focusing on missing him. She's planning for his leave at the end of the cruise in five or six months and now realizes that she can wait that long if she plans for it better. It's been four months so far, and she says that she can't remember very well at all what she even did for the first few.

January 16, 1945

All in all I'm very happy tonight. The war news is very good and makes me think that it might be over sooner than I thought. If the Russians and our men keep going at the present rate I don't see how the European end of it can go on much longer than August or Sept. of this year. The bombing of Chun King sounds good too. The news commentator tonight said that no enemy planes appeared to defend the attack. I hope this is true as the less Jap. planes I hear about the better it is with me.

She's concerned about blemishes in her skin, as are Alec and Barbara evidently. Alec has made an appointment with a doctor in Stamford for her. She knows a guy named Uri whom she "wants to look as pretty as she can for, for many years to come."

January 17th

Now Betsy is getting pretty excited. She just got three envelopes, which contained even more letters, since there were multiple days in each envelope. They cover the days between December 25th and January 4th aboard the *Enterprise*. She comments that it's OK that he can't talk about where he is, or what he's doing because then he has to talk all the more about "me, and how much you love me." Then follows three pages of pure love letter. Before that she expresses the problems involved in trying to read the letters to Barbara.

I've already read them three times and I shall probably read them three more times before the evening is over. Your threats are terrific. If you hold true to them I shall be looking at the ceiling for the next five years. I tried to read the letters to your mother. I had to skip over so much of them that we both laughed out loud. I told her that she was welcome to hear it all, but that her ears would burn. Mother agreed and said that I had better just tell Dad what I could remember and not try to read them to him. I know that if I did I'd blush a deep red. It may not be for anyone else, but I love to hear it. I feel like a beautiful, lovely, seductive girl tonight after reading your letters.

It's surprising, but I don't find his letters quite as racy as hers. I'm going to have to go back to his again and see if I've missed anything. I was actually embarrassed when I read her comment that, just like the old joke, she'd "slide down the banister to warm up dinner." Throughout her life Mom enjoyed risqué jokes, and her language could dip into the gutter when it was called for.

I find myself doing everything else but opening the remaining dozen or so letters. It still hasn't gotten comfortable, but still the letters keep drawing me closer to both of them. It's a curious mix—the excitement of being with them in these last weeks, and the sadness of knowing that I'm approaching the end. I've organized my multiple in-out boxes, dusted and polished my desk, and accidentally knocked over my coffee. I've tripled checked my email, done five or six computer chores, and so I guess it's time to dig back in.

January 18th

She tells Uri that he's perfect in every way except that he must get that one tooth fixed. It's another coincidence that throughout my young adult years I had a yellowed front tooth. It was a cheap crown after a teenage bike crash and I probably didn't get it fixed until I was Uri's age. She apologizes about going on about the tooth for fear of hurting his feelings. She says that at least he still has hair on his head. She thinks of him every minute and wonders how anyone can love someone else so much.

This envelope contains a newspaper clipping of a F6F Hellcat crashing on the flight deck of the *Enterprise*. The engine cowling is engulfed in flame. Lt. Walter Chewning has jumped up on the wing and is pulling the pilot free just in time. The fighter pilots in VF-90(N) are flying the Hellcats, and Chewning has just been awarded the Navy and Marine Corps Medal for heroism. Betsy wants to know if Uri knows the pilot. I'm sure that it was a well-known story around the ship.

January 20th

This is one of the first examples of Betsy's odd stubbornness, a trait that I came to know as she got older. It's the second time that she's mentioned not having galoshes. She was never a complainer, but in her own way exhibited the old Jewish grandmother story line: "Hey Grandma, would you like me to turn on the light there, over your chair?" "Oh that's all right, I'll just sit here in the dark."

> I took Sandy for a walk in the park yesterday. We were out for an hour and a half. We ran up and down hills and threw snowballs. My feet were almost frozen when we got back as I haven't any galoshes. I don't like to wear them so I'd just as soon have cold feet as fuss with them.

She talks about a game she plays with herself in which she sets a date until Uri's return, then counts the days, then re-sets the date it if it seems too long. She says that it sounds dumb, but for some reason she likes it. There's always news about the monthly finances and embarrassment about talking money too much. There's a cute story about a friend, Mrs. Willetts, who has a big house, two kids, and husband in the war. She washes all of the floors every day and says that she'll soon be ready for the nut house. Grandma Clara tells Betsy, "That's all right, they have plenty of floors at the nut house."

January 22nd

Betsy writes that she really doesn't even know which fleet Uri is assigned to, not to mention which task force or ship. This doesn't exactly match up with her questions about the flight deck accident with Lt. Chewning, which seems to suggest that she suspects the *Enterprise*. She received two letters dated January 6th and 7th, which means they weren't too long on the way. She loves his sexy letters and warns him that she can't wait until he can carry out all his threats and promises. She says he'll be screaming murder before she's through. She's again expressing the hope that he won't fly any more after this cruise is over and that they can settle down with their own place in Columbus. But really it doesn't matter. She'll pack up and go anywhere the Navy sends them as long as they can be together. She says, "You'll be loved and cared for as you have never been before."

We've been in Greenwich for eight days and it's a nice change of pace from the scene in Columbus, she writes. Evidently I have trouble pronouncing the word "smart." Everyone roars when I tell someone how "fart" they are. They say I'm easy to take care of and can entertain myself for hours on end. I'm impatient for Grandpa to get home from work. When he does, I attach myself to him and immediately ignore the two women.

Before I think about this any more, I feel like I need to go through all the memorabilia one more time. Everything was in two old boxes for years. Now I've sorted pictures, diplomas, wedding certificates, newspaper articles, and all those paper remembrances into Grandpa Munro's beautiful kid-leather suitcase. Each time I go through it I seem to find another little piece to the story. It's surprising that Mom and Dad's wedding album has never turned up. There must be some boxes somewhere that I haven't searched. It would be rewarding to see those photographs. I really don't have a good picture of the two of them together.

Both Uri and Betsy were bridge players. Alec and Barbara play, so Betsy teams up with her new friend Tish Lidell, who also lives in the apartment building. Tish, whom I do vaguely remember, has a boy my age. The two of us play in the living room while the adults play cards. I note some good-natured ribbing about card playing ability from Uri. He obviously thinks he's better than Betsy, but she doubts it. In her adult years my mother became a formidable player of any card game.

She was a bridge "Life Master" and could be counted on to clean out most anyone's wallet at the poker or gin table. She was scientific about it and could remember the exact play of cards from a tournament she'd played in years before.

Betsy decides to buy a nice bottle of White Horse scotch for Alec. It's evidently hard to find, and the liquor shop won't sell her two bottles unless she agrees to buy a bottle of gin as well. Barbara buys one from her to give to Alec for his birthday, and Betsy will save the second bottle for a while until she can give it to him as a present from the two of us. She's having a great visit with the Munros and has decided to stay for a month. I'm thriving in Greenwich with all the attention, and she doesn't want it to come to an end.

January 23, 1945

Last night while lying in bed I thought about the time when you first reported to Fort Schuyler. You were so excited, and meticulous with your dressing. You left with Dad, and went out into the hall and when you were standing there in the elevator you called out, "I love you Betsy." I think that's one of the sweetest things you ever did. I can still hear you saying it...

I have to fight to keep those thoughts in the back of my mind or I would be a sorry sight indeed. I shall always have those thoughts however as long as I live and am going to spend my life proving that I am worthy of them. You are the dearest, sweetest, most lovable husband in this world and I'll always thank my lucky stars that I have you...

Sandy has certainly not forgotten you because he talks about you very often.

He's always saying, "When Daddy comes home we will do this and that, etc. It's really unusual I think that he speaks of you so often. I guess I talk about you so much that he hasn't had a chance to forget.

Goodnight for now darling,
I love you.
Betsy

January 25th

A sense of relief comes over her when she receives a letter. There hasn't been one for a while, but she's feeling better because now she knows from his most recent letters that he's had a mail call or two since Christmas. She tells a cute story about me ...

I was taking a bath in Mother's bathroom when he opened the door a little ways and said, "Can I leave the door open this way so little people can come in?" When I asked who the little people were he answered "Me, naturally."

BETSY AND SANDY – 1944

*

More and more I'm becoming involved in what I have ahead of

me. Had I not decided to enter into this project it would have been much different. I would have eventually read through each of the letters, probably only once, put them away, and left it at that. As it is, I'm back in 1944-45, spending time with them over and over again. I know well the apartment in Greenwich—every piece of furniture—and can visualize being there with my grandparents. After Uri was lost we spent two weeks there every summer for the next dozen years. My mother would join me until I was old enough to take the train alone.

January 27th

Alec and I spend the day together while Betsy and Barbara take the train to go shopping in New York City. Grandma buys me a sailor suit, which I recognize in the oil painting across from my desk. The last thing I said to my mother that night was, "Can I wear my sailor suit all day tomorrow?"

She's really excited about the new nightgown and negligee she bought. "It's very scanty, pale blue satin and really gives me a good figure." She goes into great detail for half a page describing the gown. She's not going to wear it, but keep it nice, with tissue in the box, in her drawer. Every once in a while she's going to get it out, look at it, and dream of the day when she can wear it for him. It cost, "ahem, ahem, ahem $32.98." She had to borrow ten dollars from Barbara, who of course won't allow it to be paid back. Betsy laughs and says she should have borrowed twenty. She writes a little more about being careful not to roughhouse too much with the new nightie Finally she signs off at 1 a.m. saying that if she keeps writing her sexy thoughts she'll never get to sleep.

January 29th

The weather in Greenwich has turned to sleet followed by plummeting temperatures. There was an announcement on the radio for workers not to report to the Grumman aircraft plant, and in Columbus the drought has worsened. Curtis-Wright has closed down its engine plants, and people have been asked not to take baths or do laundry. Evidently the city's largest water pumps have broken down and can't be repaired until there is a significant thaw. Her parents in Columbus phoned to tell her that water pressure has dropped to almost nothing at the house. It won't reach the second-floor bathroom. But today's letter is mostly news about friends and relatives either coming back—or not coming back—from the war.

January 31, 1945

The eleven o'clock news is on now and the Russians are really going to town. I hope it isn't too long now and I don't think it will be. Probably in May or June the Germans will have accepted unconditional surrender. The Japs of course still have plenty of everything and even tho we're doing all right there's a long way to go. I wish I knew just what you were doing, where you are etc. but as it's impossible for me to know I'll have to be satisfied with the fact that you are on the carrier somewhere in the Pacific. Someday you'll be able to tell me more I hope. I would like to know if you are flying a lot. As you speak of being in the ready room so much it leads me to think that you are always on the jump ready to go at any time.

I also had a letter from Bertie. She still hasn't heard any news concerning her husband. She's the most remarkable person I've ever met. She has more courage in her little finger than I have all together. She's really a good friend too. I gave her my card and she is buying my weekly carton of cigarettes and sending them on to me. It's a good thing too because no one will sell me any here. I'm supplying Mother with her Raleighs too, and she's very grateful.

After another page proclaiming her love, she tells him that she prays for his safety every night ...

... and blow you kisses every night just as I fall off to sleep. Keep your chin up and never worry about us because we are as safe as can be. Even tho I'm lonely as heck I face each day with a smile because I know it brings us one day closer together. Right now the light is shining on my rings and they look so beautiful. I love the band and it looks so nice with my engagement ring.

Goodnight darling,
Betsy

Sandy is just fine, the apple of Dad's eye.

February 1st

Now she's scared, hasn't had a letter for two weeks, feels lost with no news. Last night she had a dream about getting a steam bath and going to the beauty parlor and being all ready for him. She wakes up just before she's to be with him—frightened and unable to get back into the dream. She has little make-believe conversations with him that mean a lot.

February 2nd

Alec and Barbara received a letter from Uri dated January 11, so now Betsy feels better. All of her incoming letters are being forwarded from Columbus, so she knows that she has mail on the way. Any interruption in mail starts the worrying process, which disappears when new mail arrives.

February 4th

Betsy receives a batch of letters from January 8th through the 15th and her anxiety disappears. She can follow the advances of the Pacific forces on the radio and knows that Manilla will likely return to the Allies in the next day or so. She envisions US troops on the Japanese mainland soon.

February 5th (second letter)

Betsy and I will be leaving Greenwich in the next week, and she wonders how Grandpa will take it. He and I have become so close that it's "hard to tell which of us enjoys it the most."

There is I realize very little news if any that you can write so I often wonder why you don't answer more of my questions and discuss a few of the things that I write about. Today I was mad when I read the following:

"Have you any plans, or gotten any ideas on what or where we will go during that time when I'm home on leave? I thought that we might go to the Adirondack Mountains or some place like that. I'm afraid that if we stay in Columbus the whole time we will just end up visiting people, etc."

What made you even write that????? You know we wouldn't stay in Columbus, you know that you must see your folks, and unless you're blind you must know that I've written time and time again of plans for that time as well as many plans for our future in general. I can remember how you used to sit down and scratch letters out in two minutes to your folks. When I read them I could tell that there was very little thought behind them. In the shortest way possible you would tell them anything on your mind. I don't feel very complimented when I see that your letters look and sound the same way now. I hate writing to you like this Uri but I do love you so

*and as I must live on letters from you
now for awhile I'd like it if you would
improve them a little. Maybe you can't
help it. I know it's tough going for you
now and that your duties require a lot
of you and are no doubt quite a strain
on your nerves. I'll probably feel like
kicking myself for writing this and worse
for mailing it but I am going to because
even tho this may shock you a little, I'll
fill the rest by telling you many sweet
true things and you'll love me again by
the time you finish reading it.*

Now that's the Betsy I'm starting to recognize. You didn't want to fall down on your obligations around her, or you'd hear about it. She does indeed follow up with two pages of love letter which I'm sure does the job.

However, keeping my eye on the timeline, I know that he's already met his fate. He never had a chance to feel her criticisms. It would have been sad to have the letters end on that note. I know what she means about some of his letters. It was easy to feel the same when I was at sea. It was hard to concentrate, and I was unlikely to fish out the letters written to me and respond point by point. I sometimes felt that the most important thing was to tell Mary Lynn that I loved her and get it in the mail. On the other hand, Betsy had time on her hands to read the letters over and over and respond in an organized way. In any case it's the first appearance of the Betsy that could be a scold. I saw it growing up, and quite simply, you didn't want to get her mad. The good part is that she'd be fun and funny ten minutes later.

February 7th

Leaving me with my grandparents, Betsy took the train from Greenwich to visit Ralph and Ginny Elmer near Rochester, New York. They were friends of Uri's from Princeton and also knew Betsy's family in Columbus. Her visit turned nightmarish, and she relates it to Uri ...

*I thought I would write while visiting
the Elmers but I didn't so this shall*

be a longer letter than usual because I shall have more to say, especially about the Elmers. Personally I think Ralph stinks and hope I don't see any more of him. I don't know what it is Uri. I really think he's ashamed of the way he dodged the draft. After listening to him talk two long evenings, I'm sure that's the case. Remember he hooked right up with the Gov't in that chemical work. Well he practically admitted that as soon as he felt safe he got out of it in order to make more money. He's scared to death that returning servicemen are going to run the country, etc. Hates the Jews and everyone else. He asked where all the boys at home were (Columbus boys) and of course as most all of them are in the service I had to say where they were etc. He soon stopped asking and said he never had much use for them anyhow. He kept saying, "Why did Uri get into it?"

I gave him every answer that I could think of but he still thinks that you did it for the uniform and the adventure. He made me pretty mad when he said there were only a few reasons why you did it, the uniform and adventure as I mentioned before, but also to get away from the house (marriage is a fairly dull proposition, he says) and to satisfy your ego. I was really mad and asked him why he had to knock others that were in when he'd been running around evading the draft himself. He admitted

*that he did but said that he would die
before he was a Pfc. or Seaman. Do you
see Uri, he is quite nutty. Virginia must
have quite a life if she listens to much
of that kind of talk. She's very nice and
kept apologizing for Ralph. She claims
she never heard him talk so bitterly in
all her life.*

It was really a relief for her to get back to Greenwich after the weekend. She missed Uri "more than she ever has before probably because without you or Sandy, I am indeed nothing." This letter is among her last. She talks at length about how fortunate she is to have Uri, and no other. One moment she's frightened, then soon she's recovered and making plans for their reunion.

My life with Grandpa is becoming closer and closer. In many ways, I've already become his little boy—we both just don't know it yet. Imagine my surprise when I read the following:

*Tonight Daddy worked a good two
hours making him a wooden violin, bow
and all, out of an old cigar box and
pieces of wood. Sandy will be thrilled to
death when he sees it in the morning.
Daddy loves to do things like that for
him and is wonderful to him.*

As mentioned earlier, I've been a musician since my days at the Naval Academy and still practice daily on the violin and mandolin. I have a very faint memory of that violin, unless it's the power of suggestion playing tricks on me. It's possible that seeing it in my mother's letter may have lit a spark somewhere in my subconscious. I do remember a cigar box violin, and now I'm re-connecting it to Grandpa. I can see him showing it to me. Could I be repainting this scene in my mind, or is it real? So many memories have bubbled to the surface since I began this project, and it's impossible to verify whether some of them are real or imagined. It's interesting that my old Scottish grandfather provided links to the violins and the fiddle music that would end up consuming so much of my life.

Alec

My grandmother Barbara's heart finally gave out in February 1959, and that June I graduated from high school in Maryland. After Barbara died, Grandpa was lonely in his Greenwich apartment. That summer he booked passage for the two of us on the *HMS Mauretania* from New York to Southampton, England. The first *Mauretania*, launched in September 1906, was the largest and fastest ship in the world. With her revolutionary steam turbines and measured speeds of twenty-eight knots, she was the pride of the Cunard Line. We traveled on her even more elegant namesake, commissioned in 1937—at the time the most luxurious of all the commercial passenger ships. She seemed huge, tied up there at the dock in Brooklyn. With a few hundred other travelers, Grandpa and I made our way up the gangplank and were shown to our stateroom for the crossing.

Alec always traveled first class, and in this part of the ship there were no other young people to be seen. Our cabin was immaculately laid out. We had beautiful beds and two writing desks with fountain pens. Clothing and shoe service was provided each day simply by leaving the items outside our door. The dining room was less than half full of its mostly elderly patrons. Airplanes were already rendering luxury ocean travel a thing of the past. I enjoyed exploring the ship and spending time with my grandfather. It was a rare experience for a seventeen-year-old, one that I especially treasure as the years go by. We spent a month in England, Scotland and Paris, where Grandpa took me to the Folies Bergere and La Rue Pigalle. When my mother later asked if we had had good seats in the French nightclubs, Grandpa replied that "we were so close that we could smell their patchoulis." I later learned that patchouli was a fragrance used in some forms of powdered make-up.

At the beginning of the trip, we got off a train together in London, up from Southampton. As we walked away from the pullman car in that cathedral-like London station, I heard a voice, thick with accent, calling from behind "Alec, Alec Munro, is that you?" Grandpa turned around and the two old men looked at each other for only a second and then embraced, wiped their tears, and began a long conversation in Russian. I was forgotten entirely as they became caught up the joy of their reunion. The man had recognized Grandpa by his peculiar walk. They hadn't seen each other in forty-four years—since playing together on the soccer fields of Russia. The other man was Igor Sikorsky, who is known for his invention of the first helicopter in 1942. I've got that slightly splay-footed walk now, and the same look in every way, and I would ponder that chance meeting in later years as I was flying Mr. Sikorsky's helicopters for Uncle Sam.

At one point Grandpa and I were riding the Underground back to Hyde Park station near our hotel. A girl my age was sitting alone a few seats ahead of us. Either she was giving me the eye or I was wishfully thinking, but as we neared our stop I asked Alec if he minded me joining him a little later at the hotel. I walked forward, introduced myself, and asked if I could join her. She was short, blonde, even more attractive up close, and told me in a German accent that her name was Christine. We visited for another fifteen minutes on the train before we arrived at her stop. I asked if I could walk her home, not believing my good fortune. We walked several blocks before she said I could accompany her no farther. I wasn't sure why, perhaps a boyfriend, but she gave me her telephone number, which I remember to this day—City 2270. The next morning I called and reached the London telephone exchange. The operator told me that almost a thousand girls worked in the building, and at least a dozen must have been named Christine. The next two days I waited at the exchange when the afternoon shift changed, hoping to see her as hundreds of girls poured out of the door. No luck. Either I had been given the brush-off, or Christine was working another shift that day. In any case, when we returned from Europe I got a card postmarked from London with the note:

"Dear Sandy, I thought you Americans were smarter than that."

Christine

I was excited that she had written me and amazed that somehow she had gotten my address in the States—until I recognized my grandfather's handwriting.

In Edinburgh, Grandpa took me to meet Norman and Isabel MacCaig. I learned later that Uri and Alec had visited them when Uri was a young boy. Norman was married to my grandfather's niece Isabel, mentioned earlier, who enjoyed a fond relationship with her Uncle Alec. Norman picked us up at Waverley Station. He was tall and thin, with balding grey-black hair, sweater vest, tweed jacket, and full of an almost manic energy. Every bit the disheveled college professor, and that's partly who he was—but more significantly— a modern Scottish poet of stature, well-known throughout a land that revers its poets as much as its football players.

From Waverly train station we sped through the narrow streets to their apartment on Leamington Terrace. I had experienced fear in taxicabs in New York City, but Norman was beyond the pale. He fully expected everyone else to stay out of his way, and somehow they pretty much did. I wasn't looking forward to our ride with him north to the Highlands the next day, and he didn't disappoint. He flew up and down the single-track roads like a madman, bouncing over tiny bridges, laughing and telling stories all the while. I don't remember much about it except the hills, the narrow roads, and Uncle Norman gesturing excitedly to us in the back seat with a cigarette in his hand, paying little attention to the road.

Somehow we survived the two days and got a glimpse of the Assynt country near Lochinver where the MacCaigs had begun to spend their summers. It is indeed mystical there in the Highlands—full of hidden lakes, flattened clouds drifting through steep valleys, and distant daggers of land jutting into the North Sea. It's easy to believe that this landscape inspired the literary nature of the Celts. Everyone we met seemed to speak in prose as pure as the burns that ripple down the mountainsides.

Grandpa didn't really appreciate Norman's poetry. "Too modern, can't make much sense of it," he said. He probably didn't appreciate Norman's pacifism either, but still helped support the MacCaigs during the war when Norman was a conscientious objector. I had the chance to visit Norman, Isabel and their family later, when the aircraft carrier *Wasp*, that I was stationed aboard, anchored near Edinburgh in 1968. As a military pilot I was incredulous that Norman had been a pacifist during the days when the Nazis were bombing London.

I remember saying, "You mean, you're actually a pacifist?"

And I also remember his response, "Well of course!"

As if—what else could anyone be? He had spent part of the war painting barracks and planting flowers at military bases, and also a year working on a government-run pig farm. When I asked him what that was like he laughed and proclaimed in his most excellent Scottish burr, "Aye, pigs are grrreat, Sandy."

*

In 1991, Mary Lynn surprised me with airline tickets to Scotland for my fiftieth birthday. We returned to Edinburgh and had our final, memorable visit with Norman. We arrived after a death-defying drive up from London. Six to eight lanes of cars and trucks, bumper to bumper at seventy-five miles per hour—the fastest lane and the steering wheel on the right. Our little rental Fiat was underpowered for the frightening task, but somehow, teeth clenched most the way, we made it. We found a rooming house just two doors down from 7 Leamington Terrace and checked in before knocking on the door at the MacCaigs. Isabel had died only a few months before and somehow we hadn't known. We'd talked to Norman by telephone before our trip, but he didn't mention his loss. He ushered us in, was disappointed that we didn't accept a cigarette, then sat down opposite us, leaned forward seriously and said,

"So tell me Sandy, just how are we related—if at all?"

SANDY, NORMAN MACCAIG, AND MARY LYNN – 1991

I knew he was joking, as we had corresponded about this visit, spent time together on my high school trip with Alec, and he knew my grandfather well. It was the funniest thing for him to say, and the rest of the weekend was the same. When Mary Lynn and I weren't sight-seeing, we spent most of our time with Norman, including enjoying a home-cooked meal prepared by his son, Euen, and his daughter, Joan. I had briefly known them as teenagers when we visited on my earlier trip with Grandpa. Norman soon remembered that he and I had hit it off well on our previous visits, and we carried on from there. He took to Mary Lynn right away, and she cooked lavish dinners for us the next two nights. He and I did the dishes together and visited until after midnight each evening—telling stories, laughing, and enjoying "just one more wee dram" of the very fine Macallan's.

Despite his pacifism, Norman was not a socialist. He had been awarded the Queen's Medal for his poetry, and in a private evening with her was most impressed with the depth of her understanding of human nature. All the same, through his writing he was a persistent thorn in the stuffier side of British society. I just came across Isabel's 1990 Christmas card in which she says, "Norman is in his eighties now with his foot down firmly on the neck of the system."

I thrill at the memory of my few brief weekends with the Mac-Caigs. Among other things he was a passable Scottish fiddler, and if inspired, could break into a beautiful Scottish tenor at the breakfast table. I needed to find a guitar to play music with him, and Euen, my cousin, provided directions to a music shop in Edinburgh where I hoped to find one to rent. When I mentioned that I needed it to play some music with my uncle, Norman MacCaig, the proprietor went to the wall, took down his very best handmade classical guitar and said, "Just take it, and bring it back whenever you like." He wouldn't even write down my name.

A vision of lifelong joy emanated from the MacCaigs. They were not well to do, but did well. Their brownstone apartment was filled with their lives. The furniture was tattered, but covered with crocheted blankets for comfort. Books were piled everywhere. As they both got older, they maintained their lifelong habit of getting up in the middle of the night to share a cigarette. Late at night we talked about Isabel being gone. Norman cried and told me that it was so hard for him to go on without her. He told me that the "well was going dry"—that the poems had almost stopped coming.

On my previous visit, when I was in the Navy, we'd be sitting talking, when out of the blue he would say, "Quick, give me a pencil and paper." He'd light up a cigarette and write out the poem. When I asked him how long it took to write a poem he said, "About the length of a fag." He seldom changed a word. They came to him as a complete thought—sometimes four or five lines, but usually much longer. Later, when Mary Lynn and I left his home to travel north, we ran into his readers and fans everywhere we went. If I told folks that Norman MacCaig was my uncle, Mary Lynn and I were invited to dinner, bought drinks, and even offered places to stay.

Norman told us that for a long time, he'd imagined Isabel as the perfect and dutiful wife of the famous poet. She would pack his suitcase for his readings around the country, which were sponsored by the Scottish Arts Council. He received a stipend for boarding trains and ferries and reading his poems each year on the mainland as well as the various Scottish isles. What Norman never suspected was that, in his absence, Isabel was writing a book. She never mentioned it until it was published. One morning she dropped a copy of the newly printed *Oxford Learner's Dictionary of English Idioms* in front of him at the breakfast table.

"With that one thump, she eclipsed everything I'd done in my life as a poet" he told me. Of course that was an exaggeration, but her

220-page book has become a primary graduate text on language usage in British universities. Isabel had a sharp wit and profound interest in language. It was just like her to work on the project for four years without telling him.

As a poet, Norman was wholly dominated by the written word. He told me that he couldn't eat a bowl of cereal in the morning without reading every word on the box, and I know what he means. I have to read during my breakfast, and I have to have an open magazine article next to the toilet, and a book in the car in case I have to wait somewhere.

"Country Dance" by Norman MacCaig, March 1969

The room whirled and coloured
and figured itself with tiny dancers.
Another gaiety seemed born of theirs
and flew like streamers
between their heads and the ceiling.

I gazed, coloured and figured,
down the tunnel of streamers —
and there, in the band, an old fiddler
sawing away in the privacy
of music. He bowed lefthanded and his right hand
was the wrong way around. Impossible.
But the jig bounced, the gracenotes
sparkled on the surface of the tune.
The odd man out when it came to music,
was the odd man in.

There's a lesson here, I thought, climbing
into the pulpit I keep in my mind.
But before I'd said "firstly brethren", the tune
ended, the dancers parted, the old fiddler
took a cigarette from the pianist, stripped off
the paper and ate the tobacco.

I remember asking Norman about that poem—he was flattered that I knew so many of his lines. He told me of the left-handed fiddler and that the poem was just exactly what happened. His poems run the gamut, but they all have a way of turning the universe inside out.

Every few months I cull another three selections from his seventeen books and send them out to friends on the *Uncle Norman Mailing List*. I get word-of-mouth requests to join the list, and so it grows month by month with people I have never met. As I think about this, I'm thankful to know that Betsy and I, in her last years, spent hours together on the phone discussing Norman's poems. I'd mail them to her then call in a week so that we could share our thoughts. She loved them as much as I did. Now I'll be reading a book, or transcribing one of Norman's poems and I'll catch myself thinking that I should call her.

SANDY AND ALEC ON THE QUEEN MARY, 1959

The trip to Europe with Alec entered its final phase as we boarded the *Queen Mary* for the six-day sail back to New York. It was even more deserted in the first-class section of the ship than a month earlier on the *Mauretania*, so I began to explore the cabin and tourist class regions. As you proceeded aft on any of the five lower passenger decks you would encounter doors with signs telling you whenever you were entering a different "class section." As a first-class passenger I could pass through all doors and go anywhere. I soon discovered a batch of raggety-tag young Brits who were emigrating to America. They were a wild and wooly lot, and I found myself spending most of my time hanging out with them, drinking beer and listening to them play music. They played jigs and reels on fiddles, pipes, a guitar and a button accordion. There were a few Irish kids, a funny cockney guy from Liverpool, and a most intriguing girl my age from Glasgow. I hadn't begun my musical life at that point, but something got it engraved on my mind during that trip. They were dancing well after midnight down in the low-ceilinged cafeteria-style restaurant, and we were a long way from first class.

After three nights of seeing Grandpa only during meals, I noticed he was being abnormally quiet. He was usually the perky old guy at dinner, telling the stories and jokes. At the end of the dinner I asked him what was wrong. He teared up a little and just smiled at me and said, "I'm just lonely, Sandy. I'm not getting to spend any time with you."

I felt like a heel. I was behaving like an unthinking adolescent, which of course I was. I vowed to spend much more time with him, which worked out pretty well. We'd read together in the afternoons, poolside, and take a swim in the ship's pool. We were in the pool one afternoon when somehow the *Queen* took a gigantic roll to port. A quarter of the water poured out of the indoor pool and Grandpa and I were sloshed around like fish in a bucket. We had been skirting a hurricane and a rogue wave took the ship by surprise. For several seconds I had visions of us going down like the Titanic. We heard rumors that the huge gyroscopic stabilizers had not yet been placed in operation. We got out of the pool and went to the salon to watch the storm. The first-class dining room had lost piles of stacked china, and a grand piano had smashed into a bulkhead. Luckily, little else had been seriously damaged and there were only a few minor injuries.

For the rest of the trip, after Grandpa went to bed in our cabin, I would go aft and party with the kids down in the tourist section. I got more closely acquainted with Kate from Glasgow, and sometimes wouldn't get back until two or three a.m., which meant that my mornings weren't too lively. Grandpa didn't seem to mind that I missed a few breakfasts. At least we were spending time together, which of course with both Uri and Barbara gone meant a lot more to him than I might have appreciated. He'd been married fifty-one years. It was a new and uncertain time in his life, and I should have been more aware of it. I now understand that loss may recede for moments in time, but it never goes away. It colors us forever.

*

Alec at seventy-nine was healthy and financially secure, but it was clear that he needed someone. Louise DeVivo became that someone, and it was easy to see she was perfect for the job. She'd had a professional life as a secretary, a successful golf career and was thirty-six when they married. Louise, forty-three years his junior, was a previous Ladies New England Golf Champion. Pretty, trim and straight-laced without being a prude, she had long been a fellow member of the Innis Arden Golf Club. She even got Grandpa to Catholic mass from time to time in his old age. He said he enjoyed it, but I got the feeling that it was just for her. She loved the old guy, and even laughed at his risqué jokes. There was no doubt that he was the man in her life. Mom and I thought it cute that Louise made it a point to leave her birth control pills out on the breakfast table.

With his love of jokes and humorous verse, Alec enjoyed that Mary Lynn and I were musicians. He got a kick out of what he considered our "old-time" lifestyle. When we hand-built our house in the Rockies, he visited each summer to check our progress. When the trusses were finally hoisted into place after three summers' work, we mixed up some cocktails from our cooler and prepared dinner there in front of the fireplace. There was no roof, but the stone buttresses, and now the trusses may have reminded him of old country inns he had known in Europe. We spread a tablecloth on a piece of plywood supported by sawhorses and grilled steaks on our newly completed stone fireplace that had taken us an entire summer to build. We sat on benches made by balancing two-by-eights on cinderblocks, and enjoyed a fantastic meal under the skeleton of our roof as the Colorado blue sky faded into evening.

ALEC, SANDY, AND LOUISE – COLORADO, 1973

Alec was proud of Louise, as well he should have been. She is not afraid to laugh, and is uncommonly good-natured. She was a devout wife until the very end, which is when I really got to know her. He loved to support her golfing events and it was easy to see that the old Scot had done pretty well for himself indeed. Earlier in their marriage I can remember my mother being suspicious of their age difference, but Betsy too was eventually won over. Now, thirty years after Alec's death, Louise and I have remained close. The two of us cared for him in the apartment during his final weeks, and I can vouch for her devotion.

*

In late January of 1978, Louise called me at the music store. We knew he'd been losing weight, and she said, "Sandy I think it's time to come see your grandfather."

That first night she picked me up at the train station when I arrived in Greenwich. It was just a mile or so up the hill, the back-town way to Harbor Heights. Because of my walks with him, I was much more familiar with the front way—two blocks down West Elm, then right on Greenwich Avenue, and downhill all the way along the shops to Greenwich Station. But that night we took the quickest way because she didn't want to leave him alone. We passed the front sides of all those houses I didn't know, dark and huddled together on the hillside above the road. Until then I had only seen their backyards from our high vantage point at Harbor Heights.

As Louise and I rode up the elevator, the sound of those cables took me back. I was beyond nervous—almost ill. I felt as if I was outside myself, watching as we nervously bolstered each other, approaching the fifth floor. He was waiting for us two steps down in the sunken living room. I knew he was waiting in that apartment and I was excited but scared to see him. Louise and I had been keeping in touch the past few weeks. She had gotten frightened and needed me to come.

What were you thinking, Grandpa? I could feel you reaching for me. I wasn't sure what to expect. Louise turned the key and I was afraid to see you. Three years before in Colorado, you were strong enough to run around and kick a soccer ball with the kids. We have the Super 8 movies. The old Scot with his maroon tam, scarf and grey wool coat chugging stiffly around the two kids, scoring goals in the thick leaves between the trees.

Key in the lock, "Munro, we're back. Oh God, Alec!" Louise screamed and sobbed. "Sandy, oh God, your grandfather."

Why hadn't I come sooner? Flying down the two steps—that damn glass coffee table with the sharp corners. "Jesus, Grandpa!" He was face down in the carpet. What are you doing? You had to get up when you heard me coming, didn't you? I couldn't say a thing, but I felt a voice calming me even as this was going on. *Do the right thing.*

Louise was electrified, her eyes panicked. "Sandy, oh God, let's get him up." And in a hurt little girl voice, "Oh Sandy, he's bleeding." We grabbed you by the arms, lifting. "Back in the chair dear ... easy, oh Alec, why didn't you just wait there for us? There was no need to get up. I told you."

"You're okay Grandpa," I said. A scrape on the forehead. "Hey, you look pretty good." You recognized me then, and probably also began to realize what had happened. "Look Louise, he's smiling." And sure enough you were.

"It's good you're here, boy," he said. And by that I know you meant Louise needs my help.

We just sat and looked at each other for a while. And I thought about that and how, in your way, you always took care of Louise. Even in your early nineties you'd make the beds and set out the breakfast table the night before. You were still repairing furniture and a variety of household items with that Goodell-Pratt Home Companion #713 tool kit you kept under your desk. I still have that nicely built maple tongue-and-grooved box with its red logo. I use the calipers, micrometer and stainless steel rule regularly at my guitar shop. The kit was made in Greenfield, Massachusetts, and you gave it to Uri in the mid-1930s.

"How about some rye old-fashioneds?" I asked, trying to sound celebratory. Though he was a Scot, Alec preferred rye to scotch.

"We could all use one," Louise replied, and I could see you nodding approval.

"I suppose that this would be a pretty illogical time to give up your evening rye, Grandpa," I added.

Louise cleaned you up as I searched about for the bitters and syrup. I couldn't imagine the next days or weeks. This was just the arrival. I was apprehensive, but also full of certainty that this was what I should be doing.

We sat down near your chair, Grandpa—it's coming back to me in slow motion. Your skin was almost translucent, every vein clear-ly visible and the bleeding wouldn't' stop. Mostly from the arm and forehead—just a little, but it wouldn't stop. Your skin was mottled and scalloped as if it could scarcely contain you much longer. Louise stuck on a few small bandages, and we raised our glasses together.

I knew that I should make a toast, but before I could think of any-thing Louise said, "Well Alec, here's to your first fall."

In a slow tired voice he replied, "And I wun be takin' miny more o' them, I kin be tellin' ya."

The rye was bringing the old guy back to life, and with it his brogue. I would see times like this often during the first week. Alec laughing and telling stories, and if I didn't think about it—he looked now, with the life in him, almost like he could be around for years. Before the last year or so he always weighed 170 pounds, "never more, never less," he liked to say. He has lost weight now and his once square-shouldered physique has folded inward.

After the frightening beginning, we shared another memorable din-ner. What a wonderful evening it turned out to be—a nice, simple meal that Louise had started before picking me up at the station. Peas, thinly sliced roast beef, along with potatoes and of course a slice of white bread. Grandpa was himself again.

The three of us sat around after dinner relaxing, and I filled Grandpa and Louise in on our life in Colorado. For the previous six years I'd been teaching physics and math at Aspen High School while Mary Lynn and I spent the summers building the house. We had moved in two years before—into the shell of it anyway. Alec and Louise hadn't been out West since our open-air dinner in front of the fireplace in 1973. Now it was five years later and my school teaching days were behind me. There was a chance to become fully involved in music for the first time.

I played in a bluegrass band and had bought Rick Barlow's funky little guitar shop for ten thousand dollars. *The Great Divide* was up the stairs, down a hallway and directly above a real estate office. The whole shop was half the size of a school bus, with room for only thirteen guitars on the wall. Rick was a good craftsman, especially in that '70s barnwood style. He had some beautiful antique cabinets, handmade instruments, and the store was tastefully done. Old-time fiddle and banjo music often permeated the offices below, but evidently didn't enhance the real estate experience. A few weeks after I bought the store from Rick, I acquired the first electric guitar and amp. Shortly thereafter it was mutually agreed that I should find a new space. We moved to a new shop on Monarch Street, a perfectly suited turn-of-the-century brick building with twice the amount of room. I had been sending pictures to Grandpa and Louise of *The Great Divide*, and even now, he was interested in knowing all about it.

*

After dinner we decided to play a few hands of crazy eights, as we had for years. We cut the cards for the deal, laughing and having a fine time. Grandpa was right there—it could have been years earlier. I drew a deuce, Louise a ten, and we handed the cards to Grandpa. He stopped smiling then, and without looking at the cards, cut straight to the ace of spades. I felt a chill crawling up my back—Louise and I just looked at each other.

The second night we went to the Clam Box for dinner. A storm blew up and Grandpa seemed to really enjoy the excitement of us getting him to the car. I got food poisoning later that night with a complete case of stomach cramps and sweats. The wind blew rain horizontally, and it felt like I was in some crazy nightmare where I was dying and Grandpa was taking care of me. I kept having to throw up, and those forty-year-old single-paned windows just leaked and whistled. The lightning flashed ghostly images of the Greenwich skyline on the bedroom wall. The siren on the fire station now seemed threatening and otherworldly. A Russian city appeared in my dreams—its minarets somehow mixed with Edinburgh Castle flashing in lightning, perched high on jutting stone cliffs.

Alec didn't seem to have much breath left for talking, and a lot of times we just sat with him while he looked out the kitchen window. I could tell he was enjoying himself. He breathed slowly and easily, and dozed off from time to time. After our lunch, usually soup and bread, he would perk up for a while, and sometimes for twenty minutes or so would be completely engaged. It was a little hard to understand him —he had that funny way of saying "yah" on the in-breath. It was a thing about Grandpa, besides his brogue—his way of answering you on the in-breath. If you finished asking him a question that required a "yes" answer, your timing was critical. If he was getting ready to breathe inward, that's how he would answer. A sort of a backwards, percussive, puff of a "ya." In his last few days it was a mainstay of his conversation. Just recently I've noticed the same mannerism among older Cape Breton folks, so it must be a Scottish thing. He still had a big, wide laugh, which gave us a chance to see those fantastic teeth. They were all original, as he was happy to point out, but looked like often-repaired antiques. Different shades of browns and yellows mostly, but not rotten looking, or even unattractive.

"But Sandy, ninety-four years is a bloody goddamn awful age to live to," he would say. "All my friends died twenty years ago."

"I know what you mean, Grandpa." I said, "All except your forty-nine-year-old wife."

We'd both laugh. They had been married sixteen years now, and had spent a good part of that time traveling the world—always playing golf. Now we sat in the evening by the window and talked of the funny coincidences in our lives together.

Sometimes he would be right there, and other times he'd say, "I'm well on my way, Uri. I'm glad you're here, boy."

Uri was Grandpa's only son—and now the old man could not, or maybe saw no reason, to keep us straight. Until that time, I had always thought of death as an instantaneous thing. Now you're alive, now you're not. But it isn't. He kept going part way out, and then coming back. I remember asking if he reminisced much.

He was barely breathing, with his eyes lightly closed, and after a while said, "Right now I'm a young man playing football in Russia." He was more than ready to go, and expressed surprise when he kept waking up each morning.

These events confirm a certain destiny for me now. Grandpa and I were born half a century and an ocean apart, but have been connected by an evolutionary thread that makes us alike in ways that I never imagined. Not only that we look alike, but I knew him well enough to feel him creeping into the way I think about things. Something very comforting in small routines, sameness.

Louise was a fine-humored nurse and wife those last weeks. She did whatever had to be done and loved old Alec just fine. We really didn't know just what we could do for him other than be there and make him comfortable. He was easy on us, as it turned out. He didn't ask for much. I could tell that our world was becoming more dreamlike to him, and that the other place he was visiting was also a comfort.

"What are you thinking about, Grandpa?" I asked.

After breathing slowly, "It's a fine day to be skiing here with you, Uri."

"I can almost be there with you, Grandpa," I responded, and in fact had been skiing all day with him on my mind a week before. Even before this week of caring for him with Louise, I felt that he was with me a lot of the time.

Old age was sure something he was getting to know all about right now. There were big bruises on his arms from being lifted in and out of his wheelchair, and his face would cut easily if he scratched it. Louise kidded him about how we'd have to put on the little mittens to keep him from scratching, and he'd acknowledge her with a look of understanding. It took more and more wind for him to talk now, and he didn't try unless he had something he really wanted to say. He knew that we were with him, though, and he with us. His eyes would still tear up when Louise or I would trigger certain memories. I seemed to make more and more of a transformation to Uri in his eyes. And yet by what he said, I knew it was my life he was thinking about most of the time.

Louise had also undergone a transition to Barbara, and neither of us felt it made much sense to correct him.

"How're you feeling, Munro?" Louise would ask after dinner.

"No complaints, Barbara," he'd reply, and that was pretty much the story.

He really was "well on his way" now, and it was nothing to complain about. Nothing but the food, anyway. We thought he was just being fussy. For the first three or four days, we'd cut whatever we were eating into the smallest of bites. That was fine for a while, but then he decided we should only set a spoon at his placemat in the future. Forks were too hard to handle now, and he recognized they were becoming dangerous for him. So a spoon it was, and I went shopping for a small blender. At first, Grandpa took interest in the food preparation, and gave us instructions on what to put in the blender. As it turned out, we only blended for a few days before we switched to baby food. We got every kind of Gerber's we could find so that he'd have a nice selection. At first it was mostly vegetables, but then in the last days he wanted only fruit. It was the reversed progression of an infant, who likes only fruits, then learns to accept the vegetables. Grandpa was going the other way.

The days went by slowly, each like the one before but with a lessening of conversation. He seemed to level off in a place where he might spend the next two or three weeks. I've always felt terrible that I left before he died, and if I'd stayed another four days it wouldn't have worked out that way. For a long time I regretted my decision to leave. I had an active but struggling new business back home, and no one to take my place. Now, re-reading Louise's words, I can feel comforted that they had that time alone. She expressed it beautifully in her letter mailed just a week after he was gone.

A Day in my Life with Alec

I'd wake up in the morning and look over at his bed. Usually he was awake and would smile and say, "Hi." Always a cheery "hi," never any aches or pains. If I decided to arise with him, he would sit by my bed and say, "Stay there another five minutes until you've awakened. Meantime I'll shave." Or if I had overslept, he would be in the living room reading his New York Times, waiting for me with the table all set for breakfast. He never ate without me.

He was never bored, he was never boring. If he didn't know what to do he would go to his encyclopedia. He was clever with his hands; make doll furniture, hook a rug, upholster a chair, repair my salad fork. He kept his tools in order, his clothes in order, mended his socks and pants too. He could cook. He would help me with anything and if I interrupted him for something, he never became angry or upset. He bought me anything I wanted. He never said no to me. He loved to watch me play golf and was thrilled if I pulled off a finesse shot.

When he was in the wheelchair he put his hand on my arm and said, "We've had many happy years together." He often told me what a good person that I was, and that I was a beautiful woman. I often told him that he had a nice shaped head, and that he was a handsome man.

When he died, it was just the two of us in the apartment. I'm so glad of that. His breathing finally got shallow and I held his hand and got down on my knees and prayed to the Lord to have mercy on this good man. And reading Christina Georgina Rossetti's "Song"—"When I am dead, my dearest, sing no sad songs for me." He liked that poem, and was trying to tell me, through it, that it's OK if I remember him, and OK if I forget. How could I forget when he was so good to me? He was far gone and could not hear me or know I was sobbing so. I watched the little pulse on his neck get fainter and fainter till it stopped. That wonderful body and spirit that had lived for 94 years, and no matter what happened, could come up smiling.

Louise Munro, March 16, 1978

For the first few years after he was gone, I kept feeling that he was still watching over me somehow, making sure that I was doing right. I'd be working outside, and he would pop into my head. Or someone would say something and it would remind me of him, or I'd use words or expressions, and realize they were his. Now, having re-read Louise's letter, I'm with him again.

Completely by coincidence, the day after Alec died, Chris Cassatt came across the street to my music shop and handed me the damnedest gift. Chris is a talented photographer/cartoonist who produces the comic strip, *Shoe*, and worked for *The Aspen Times*. His wife, Lauren, had been visiting northern Scotland and brought back for me a recent edition of the *Munro Clan Newsletter*. The front page displayed Colonel Patrick Munro, chief of the clan. He was ninety years old, and goddamn it looked just like Grandpa standing there. She also included our family crest mounted on a silvered kilt pin, with our frightful clan motto, "Dread God."

Uri

Now, reading Uri's letters, I'm glad to have served during the last days of the World War II warships. It gives me an accurate picture of his life, two decades earlier, aboard the *Enterprise*.

At sea, I lived in the forward-most "stateroom" on the *USS Wasp*. Commissioned in 1943, this was the ninth *Wasp* to serve the US Navy. Except for the captain's bridge and the squadron ready rooms, there was no air conditioning in these World War II boats. My tiny cubicle with its thin metal door and built-in rack was subject to significant temperature variation. It could be a foul-smelling, noisy place because it was only one bulkhead away from the fo'c's'le—a big below-deck space just under the bow where painting, varnishing, and repair were always going on. Lines and deck tools hung on the bulkheads. The twin twenty-five-ton anchors were situated in huge steel deck mounts along with the chain, capstan and windlass necessary to raise and lower them through the four-foot hawseholes. Each link of the chain weighed more than three hundred pounds.

The fo'c's'le was also the working and non-working hangout of the bosun's mates. These are the guys you visualize when you think of sailors. They mopped, scraped, painted, rigged and maintained the ship. They stood watches, manned the helm, and served on emergency crews. At any given time, day or night, I was serenaded by young "bosuns to be" as they diligently learned to play their bosun's pipes—a melodically limited instrument if there ever was one. These seamen, called "deck apes" by some, proudly wore their pipes on thin chains around their necks as part of their uniform. It was not so much an instrument, but a three-inch pipe with a hole over a small bowl on one end. With your right hand, you could essentially slide between two notes and eventually learn to play the specific "calls." There was some skill involved in executing them properly, not unlike learning to play a simple flute. Announcements of any kind over the public address system were preceded by an identifiable whistle from the pipe. On a noisy ship underway, the "bosun's call" would alert the proper parties to pay attention to the upcoming message.

I was practicing guitar and banjo in my little grey room whenever I had the time. Sailors would often stop by and ask if they could listen for a while. They'd visit and if I saw a bosun's pipe hanging around their neck I'd point at it, laugh, and tell them to keep practicing. It was coveted duty to be the sailor who actually blew the pipe calls and made the announcements that would be heard throughout the ship.

The anchors and chains put up a deafening roar and vibrated through the metal decking under my compartment, but that only happened upon entering and departing anchorage. The real problem was the steam catapults, one of which was only a few feet over my head as I tried to sleep in my often churning rack. From the flight deck the catapult looked like a three-hundred-foot metal zipper. The plane's nose wheel gear connected to a harness, which was connected to a huge steam-powered piston below the deck.

During flight operations, each catapult fires every minute or so. Imagine the power of a piston that has to pull a 30,000-pound airplane from zero to 120 knots in four seconds. A massive water brake would slow the piston just after launch. The whole "cat shot" was a gigantic kerrrr-thunk. The "kerrrr" four seconds long, and the "thunk" feeling as if a truck had smashed into a bridge abutment next to your head at seventy miles per hour. Imagine now sleeping fifteen feet directly below the center of that piston. It's amazing what you can get used to. After a week or two at sea, the crashing vibrations, noise, pitching and rolling had a way of lulling me to sleep. It was a way to escape.

I was less than seventy feet from the bow of the Wasp, and the vertical motion in a North Atlantic storm is at first alarming. As the bow struggles upward, you're pushed hard into your thin mattress. Then you're almost weightless on the way down—the shuddering starts as you're pressed hard into the bunk upon rising again. This could continue for hours, or even days on end. I remember tightly gripping my rack's frame, paranoid as the old ship strained and groaned.

We'd studied metal fatigue at Annapolis and the basics are not hard to understand. Bend a wire (or a beer can) back and forth enough times and it gets hot, then breaks. Thirty years of storms, battles, kamikaze and torpedo attacks had long since begun that process on the *Wasp*. The old clunker sounded like it was coming apart at the seams, but after a while I could sleep right through it. There certainly wasn't anything you could do about it anyway.

My desk job, as a junior officer in Helicopter Anti-Submarine Squadron Eleven, was to run the avionics department. Our primary job as pilots was to know our aircraft, its mission, and to fly day or night, but we had collateral administrative jobs too. I really didn't run the department, and didn't really do much at all except sign the occasional stray piece of paperwork. My chief petty officer knew what to do, and that I was essentially unnecessary. From his twenty-year point of view, I was green behind the ears anyway.

The avionics shop was far aft in the ship at the rear end of the hangar deck near the fantail, but thirty feet up a ladder (stairway) just below the overhead (ceiling). From the top of the ladder, just under the overhead, you were standing on a grated steel platform. If you looked toward the bow, your eyes were lined up just below the top of three large hangar bays end-to-end—you could sight forward seven hundred feet over the tops of the ship's parked aircraft. In storms, the forward section of the bay would be twisting left, while the aft section twisted to the right. This rotation was significant—it seemed like ten degrees, although I'm sure it wasn't, and had been happening year after year. In a North Atlantic storm, green water could wash across the bow, sixty feet above the waterline. Scary. I knew the ship was designed to flex in three independent sections for just this reason, but somehow it didn't make me feel any better.

In addition to their naval mission, the SH-3A Sea Kings were used as the presidential "helo" throughout the 1970s and '80s. At sea we flew with a crew of four, trying to track Russian submarines as well as taking on the variety of missions assigned to helicopters. We delivered and picked up mail from other ships in the task force. Often we'd be called upon to transfer critical medical cases off smaller ships, or perform search and rescue. It was exciting to be in a hover, forty feet over the fantail of a destroyer that was being assaulted by twenty-foot waves. The ship's masts out ahead of you were swinging back and forth though the air—you didn't want to get too close. A crew on the deck below would attach the rescue chair to the hoist cable while your own crewman guided the frightened and sometimes injured party slowly upward and into the hatch. It took experience and relaxed hands on the flight controls to avoid slamming your subject into the rigging, or getting him hung up on a railing.

Shipboard life hadn't changed much on these boats, even since the World War II days. I know what it's like to return to a ship the size of a postage stamp in an endless choppy sea. Up close, the ship tosses and turns, deck slick from oil and sea spray. It's a hard-to-see, moving platform and on a dark night makes you wonder why anyone would do it at all. Training is a matter of putting together a sequence of skills and then doing them over and over again while introducing ever more dangerous variations. Add darkness, add a pitching deck. The landings and tie-downs were especially unsettling. Four to six helicopters would follow each other down the glide path and land about ten seconds apart. The deck crew would chain down the first chopper then run back quickly to the next. That was your moment of instability. Your own main rotor blades were spinning horizontally only a few feet from the tail rotor blade of the aircraft ahead of you. Tail rotors spin six times faster than the main rotor, vertically, just in front of your windshield. If the deck was pitching and slippery, the smallest slide forward would result in a catastrophe that you couldn't think about. Routine events were dangerous enough that mistakes just couldn't be made.

Unlike the *Enterprise* with its hydraulic catapults, the *Wasp* had been upgraded to steam cats, and an angled flight deck. The angle gave fixed-wing aircraft a chance to go around again if its tail hook missed the arresting gear cable. It also kept planes from plowing into a net barrier, or parked aircraft on the bow, in the event of a botched or emergency landing. Still, the *Wasp* was a World War II boat, and not very different at all from CV-6, the *USS Enterprise*. She was mothballed in 1972, only four years after I left her. Shortly thereafter, with great ceremony, she was decommissioned and, as commonly said in the Navy, "made into razor blades."

*

In the months before Uri and his squadron embarked on Christmas Eve of 1944, he knew he would soon become part of an existing legend. The ship had been involved in nearly every storied battle in the Pacific—luckily missing Pearl Harbor by only a few days. She was steaming toward Honolulu, less than twenty-four hours out, when 353 diving planes from six Japanese carriers swarmed Oahu that Sunday morning. The raid heavily damaged eight of our battleships and changed for all time the role of the US Navy at war. Without the battleships, the carrier was unexpectedly brought to the forefront as America waged war in the Pacific. Beginning with her attacks on submarines immediately following December 7, 1941, the *Big E* had been crucial in the Battle of Midway, the raids on the Marshall-Gilbert Islands, Wake Island, Marcus Island, Guadalcanal, the Solomons, Santa Cruz, Truk, New Guinea, the Mariana Turkey Shoot, Okinawa, Formosa, and Leyte Gulf, for a total of twenty Battle Stars of the twenty-two awarded in the Pacific Theater. Uri was joining a team that had suffered devastating attacks, but had inflicted far greater damage on the enemy. There's obvious pride in his letters, although he still isn't allowed to mention the name of his ship.

To the Japanese, the *Enterprise* had a reputation for being impossible to find, though she seemed always nearby—and on the attack. Twice in the early part of the war the enemy reported her sunk, which worked in her favor. A prime target of massive and sustained air attacks, she often made the critical difference—her aircraft projecting power hundreds of miles in any direction. She could pinpoint her explosive flying armada like a missile to a target. It was no accident that by 1944 the *Big E* was so effective. The entire ship, with its crew of two thousand, was a hardened machine. She had fought since the beginning and the men were intensely proud of their role in the war, which had finally turned their way. There was work yet to be done, and intense battles remaining, but our carrier task forces, often led by CV-6, were taking it to the enemy.

THE *BIG E* UNDER DIVE BOMBER ATTACK IN THE BATTLE OF SANTA CRUZ

Because I was assigned to the Atlantic fleet, I was never in a war zone aboard the *Wasp*, but I do know that adrenalized feeling. Even a rescue could get your blood pumping. There were always unknowns. You could be launching on a dark rainy night, knowing you would not be seeing a single thing past your cockpit windshield for the next four hours. We chased Russian subs around until they surfaced so that we could take intelligence photos. It was the Cold War and there was always the feeling that they might start something. And you almost wished they would.

Now looking back, it feels a little more like rival bullies pushing each other around in the schoolyard. It had to be a far cry from the charged emotion of the *Enterprise*, full of airplanes and pilots, steaming into one battle after another. The anti-aircraft gunners scarcely had time to sleep. Aircrews were flying shifts around the clock. The kamikaze attacks, so far unable to locate the *Enterprise*, were becoming more frequent and deadly for the rest of the fleet. And all along, the analogy of a floating city is apt. There was a ship to run, with its complicated array of logistical support: three meals a day in a variety of mess halls, refueling, resupplying and rearming. Everything that happened existed to support flight ops, and the *Big E* was launching and recovering aircraft almost continually.

I'd been foolish to think that I'd read these letters once and that would be it. It would have been impossible to comprehend the whole picture. To do that, I need to be coordinating the squadron's and ship's chronicles with the letters. I need to keep diving into them, along with the maps, over and over again. Google Maps make it faster. I can see the straits leading into Leyte Gulf, for example, and why, a few months before, it had been a strategic necessity to intercept the enemy and protect our landing forces on their way to Manilla. It's easy to tell that the enemy-occupied China coast isn't that far away, and a task force with dozens of ships can cover a surprising distance when you factor in the reach of its aircraft. You can be doing battle one day in the southern Philippines and engaged the next in Formosa, a thousand miles away.

Hadley's journal confirms that in the beginning of January the fighters have had a week of contact. Casualties have been light even though the Hellcats have been returning pretty shot up. A few landing accidents and a mid-air collision have cost VF-90 three good fighter pilots. Two Japanese Dinahs were shot down as they approached the task force, and other enemy planes were driven off. At this point the *Enterprise* is to avoid all enemy contact unless she happens to stumble upon the main Japanese fleet. Her tasks are to cut the enemy supply routes through the Philippines, Formosa, and along the South China coast, and whenever possible not to disclose her position.

January 12th marks Uri's first actual combat mission. He's flying with Kippen, his skipper, as they encounter a Japanese convoy in Kanfong Bay on the China coast. They're excited to discover a light cruiser, four destroyers, four destroyer escorts, and six smaller ships in the bay far below.

> *The TBMs took off with four 500-pound bombs each. The already poor weather grew worse all day. Ceiling and visibility closed in, and the wind and sea kicked up as a typhoon churned westward across the south end of the China Sea. Enterprise bombers and fighters, in company with a similar group from the Independence, skimmed northwestward between gray clouds and a gray sea, a few hundred feet off the water, turned into the coast*

and followed its dark, irregular contour north for another twenty miles before they found the fifteen ship convoy, steaming due north in two parallel columns across the spacious bay south of Quinhon.

Over the target the base of the dark gray overcast was at 4000 feet and visibility was at ten miles or better. Mat Gardner's night hawks swarmed in for the kill, delighted and relieved to have targets that they could see and a chance to inflict damage that could be observed and reported. Lieutenant Russell Kippen, CO of VT-90, led the attack and picked the strongest target, the Katori-class light cruiser. His TBMs followed him in, attacking at once from south to north with no circling or maneuvering for position. Kip's two bombs straddled the cruiser, close aboard on both sides, and she turned to port, heading for the beach. Joe Jennings put two of his bombs into a destroyer which also headed for shore, burning and under heavy strafing attack by the fighters. Jim Landon missed on his first run, but on his second run hit one of the merchantmen on the stern. The merchantman, already holed by two of Fighting 90's rockets, settled heavily, black smoke sloping downward at a 45-degree angle.

When the night birds, with the forward-pointing Enterprise arrow outlined on their tails, joined up under the low clouds to seaward for the flight home, one merchantman was down, two were dead in the water, burning and settling, two more were wounded and heading for shore, and another two were hit and circling aimlessly.

— Edward P. Stafford, *The Big E*, p.489

All of the pilots return safely, some with flak damage—but now the aircrews are sky high. They have finally entered the maelstrom that will engulf every waking moment of their lives for the next five months. The *Enterprise* was two hundred miles south of the tip of Indochina, sixty-odd miles from the coast, moving north with its task force, attacking targets of opportunity on the south China coast—intensely on the lookout for the Japanese fleet they suspect is nearby.

Now the narrative is becoming so tightly woven that I need to keep comparing Hadley's journal and other sources with my father's letters.

Multiple readings and jumping back and forth are the order of the day. This obviously isn't a narrative of Torpedo 90, or of the *Enterprise*, but rather an attempt to get closer to my family story.

Before me I have Uri's daily letters dated from January 13th to January 20th.

January 13, 1945

I'm sitting in the ready room in between times getting off this letter.

Yesterday was a pretty busy day for your little boy. I was out with Kippen a good part of the day getting some work done, and during the night just before I stayed up all night, all ready to go, so I missed out on considerable sleep. However, I got all my sleep caught up on now, and I am in reasonably good shape.

*

I used to enjoy the ready room environment. Besides the camaraderie, it had big reclining leather seats with headrests and a swing-up desk. Other than the captain's bridge, forward con, and the radar room, it was one of the few air-conditioned spaces on the ship. You could usually kick back and z-out for a while if there wasn't a brief or debrief going on. There was always hot coffee, and pilots playing gin or acey-ducey. On one four-month cruise, fellow pilot, and my Naval Academy roommate, Doc Wright and I played gin rummy for a penny a point almost every day. We kept totaling the score and I owed him seven cents the day we sailed back to Boston.

In some ways it's getting easier for me to read the letters at this stretch, even though there are quite a few passages relating to me. I've been pretty close to it all for the past year and I'm getting to feel a little more like I know my dad. He was twenty-eight—the same age as I was at the end of my naval career. So many age inversions in this project. I'm trying to think of Uri as my father when in fact he's fourteen years younger than my son. And even though I'm closer now to seventy than sixty-five, it's still not impossible to inhabit the little boy who was also at the center of these letters.

I began this project with the idea of getting to know my dad, and it's true that I'm getting a feel for his personality. In reading and re-reading his letters I'm so much reminded of myself at his age, and even more so of my son. Alex, named after his great-grandfather Alec, mirrors Uri's idealistic and accepting nature. As I read the letters, flashes of my son Alex keep playing before me. Uri believes unfailingly in his cause. There is no ambiguity, no uncertainty. His letter to the *Columbus Dispatch* before the war sheds some light:

> *The young men of America would do well to heed the words of Colonel Lindbergh. His judgment and honesty, as well as his patriotism have never been questioned. His perception and understanding of military matters are shown in his high rating of the German military machine some time ago.*
>
> *Certainly our hearts and hopes are with the Allies and all they stand for. But—we are doing them more harm than good by our childish hysteria and loose talk. We are in the position of holding the loser's coat and yelling, "Come on, let's get up and fight!" every time he gets knocked down. Instead let us put ourselves in the position of big brother to the loser, someday strong enough to subdue the neighborhood bully.*
>
> *The way to this goal is to follow Lindbergh's suggestion —stop fooling the Allies by sending them talk and a few second-hand planes. Instead prepare to dominate and defend this hemisphere with the best air force, mechanized divisions and navy in the world.*
>
>
>
> *Uri A. Munro*
> *Columbus, Ohio*
>
>

There was something curious about this letter until I began to read more about Charles Lindbergh. He was in fact an isolationist, and crusaded against getting involved in the war in Europe. Why would Lindbergh take this position? There were two sides to the story. Yes, he had twice visited Germany and reviewed its aircraft-manufacturing capabilities—and yes, he was presented a medal by Goering at the behest of Adolf Hitler. But even after Hitler had suffocated Poland, Lindbergh believed that we ultimately had much more to fear from the "Semi-Asiatic" Russians. His hope was that the Allies could support

Hitler, who would then defeat the communists on their march west. Hitler wouldn't live forever and the German people would outgrow their human rights violations.

In hindsight it's hard to imagine how any prominent, well-educated hero with the stature of Charles Lindbergh could have accepted the aggression of the Third Reich. Some are convinced of a racial motivation. In any case he was practical enough to believe that we'd better get prepared. When he returned to America after his second trip he did indeed deliver strong, specific suggestions for beefing up our military air power in response to the German aviation program. He pointed out that if nothing were done, Hitler would quickly surpass every other nation in the building of combat aircraft.

Most significant for me is that Uri's letter is a political statement that he obviously felt strongly about. I have a folder file in my desk, brimming with evidence of my similar leanings. My son sees the world as a Republican and so I perceive myself sandwiched between two conservative generations. Truthfully, there is no reason to interpret Uri's politics either way. There is zero mention of the word in any of the letters. It was all black and white in 1945, but is now spliced with every shade in between. My son, working hard in the high-tech business world, sees no real danger ahead—new energy sources will appear, the world will not overheat, science will cure all, the banks will not rob us blind. Make money and enjoy it. I admire his celebratory stance in the face of events that scare skeptics like myself. In his time, Uri lived in a world of no contradiction. He had a world to save, and his generation was united to save it. That put him right where he needed to be.

I'm finding now that there is something I've been missing. I've gone back to reread *The Big E,* which I read years ago as a midshipman. I keep thinking of Uri as a heartsick young officer separated from his family, and certainly that was a big part of it. But there is another side—the excitement that comes with this dangerous and all-consuming mission. Now I'm feeling disappointment that he really got to do so little of what he was there for. Until the letters I had always thought of him as being gone for a long time, fighting in the great Pacific war, but that's not the way it was. The training took almost two years, some of which included being with Mom and me, but he had barely entered the battle.

As I read *The Big E*, I can see there is a continuity to the struggle. Heroes have come and gone, and some of them fight on through much of the war. Uri's skipper and pilot is one of these. His combat involvement began long before my father joined the ship. I can sense confidence in the letters now. Uri is excited to be doing what he signed up for. Fear has been pushed aside by the exhilaration and resolve they're all feeling. Betsy's focus is entirely on their relationship and raising me. For her, the family might be the center of it all, but Uri is being absorbed by the matters at hand. He shares Kippen's confidence in the air. They've been crewmates since mid-September during their BOQ Dog days in Hawaii, and now they fly together full time.

I need to read those January letters from Uri again. Could there be something else? In re-reading, it's all determination. If any fear or premonition exists, I can't spot it. His spirit is high. No matter how dangerous it gets, you can never think of yourself as the one who doesn't come back.

Task Force 38 is on the move, ranging from Hong Kong to points north along the China coast, and searching between Formosa (now Taiwan), and the Pescadores. The squadrons are sent out on sector searches and any discovered enemy units are to be attacked.

On January 16th, eight Avengers led by Kippen are sent to destroy any and all possible Japanese installations at Pratas Reef. The sky is overcast at seven hundred feet but lifts to one thousand as they approach the island. The skipper, with Uri in the back seat, flattens the concrete radio station and the rest of the planes mop up the remaining buildings, including some nearby grass huts. The only edifices left standing are a small painted Shinto shrine, and a large three-holed outhouse. One of the pilots discovers and blows up an ammo dump. Under darkening skies, they head back to the ship along with their four fighter escorts.

It's almost anticlimactic reading Uri's last letters. He's going along fine. Somehow I expect him to be foreshadowing his final flight with some psychic apprehension of what is going to happen. Nothing is out of the ordinary—why should it be? He's working hard, doing his job, and biding his time.

The ship is being tossed about at the edges of a typhoon and for the first time he gets seasick. His body aches, his stomach is upset, and he has a splitting headache. He takes a few aspirin in the middle of the day, lies down and wakes up five hours later feeling good enough to write a four-page love letter. They're in the storm three more days, but now his seasickness doesn't bother him any more.

January 17, 1945

... The longer I'm out here, the more I miss you sweetheart. I'm sure going to pull every trick I know to stay by your side in the good old USA after I get back. Just having you and Sandy with me I won't care if we live in the middle of the desert. We'll make it home, and we'll make it fun. Anyplace with you around would be fun dear, and without you, no matter how nice the place might be, it is dreary and empty. Waikiki Beach in Honolulu, with Diamond Head in the background would be very pretty, but it's just a beach to me. On the other hand, the beach at Corpus Christi and Jacksonville stand out, because you were there to make them live in my memory.

Love, Uri

Thursday, 18 January 1945

The weather continues bad. The vertical displacement from trough to crest of the sea running at present must be between twenty and thirty feet. Our bunks seem to rise and fall at least twice that far. The only air operations were routine fighter CAPs of four planes at a time. Landing in such weather is a breathtaking sight. Rain whips across the deck, driven by a forty-knot wind and the deck itself rises and falls twenty to thirty feet. The LSO (Landing Signal Officer) brings the planes in high and fast and they dive straight for the deck when they get the cut. Naturally some of these landings are extremely rough and tires are frequently blown.

Stories of the damage caused by the storm are coming in from other ships of the force. The San Jacinto, a CVE, rolled so severely that she lost eleven planes over the side when the tie-down lines carried away. A CVE lost eleven planes when her flight deck was all but torn away by the fury of the waves. In our Big E, one of the weather curtains on the hangar deck was smashed in, crushing the wing of a TBM, and a spare engine broke loose and ended up in number two elevator pit, after spinning about the deck.

— from Hadley's VT(N)-90 squadron history

The rolling deck contributed to the landing accidents, and the storm still shows no chance of abating. There are a few more of Uri's letters bunched together. The last is dated January 20th—nothing to indicate tension from the combat flights he's been involved in. He just calls it "getting some work done."

*

It may seem strange that I've had the letters for over a year and I'm just now finishing reading them. But I wanted to stay in real time as much as possible. There are still the rest of the unopened ones from Betsy to contend with, and more memorabilia to dig out of Grandpa Munro's leather suitcase. I've been through it all before, but somehow keep discovering new things—letters from Uri or Betsy's other friends, and photographs that didn't fit the story until I understood it all a little better.

I was pulled away from this writing project a few weeks ago by Barry Smith. He writes the humor column "Irrelativity" for *The Aspen Times* and is starting to get noticed on the national stand-up comedy circuit. He's a good friend, fellow musician, very funny, and has asked me to participate in an evening of storytelling at the theater in Aspen. There will be nine of us, each with eight to ten minutes to tell our story. No notes can be used, and I'm sure that I'm the only one who will be telling a sad story. We know that most will be funny, but Barry thinks that I should talk about my father and the letters. The thought of it scares me, even though I've fronted bands for years and am quite comfortable talking to an audience through a microphone. On the other hand, forcing myself to accept his invitation will put pressure on me to proceed with this work. It needs to be done, and by publicly committing to it I have made a deal with myself that is a little harder to back out of.

It is easy enough to feel apprehensive. I consider Barry's invitation from all angles for a few days and decide I will not do it. I use the excuse of not needing to feel any more pressure in my life than I already feel. I call Barry before his advertising deadline to turn him down. I am relieved. The pressure is off, and now I can continue my slow drift through the process of reading the letters and writing about them.

Naturally, I soon start to feel guilty about my withdrawal and begin to wish that I hadn't chickened out. That's really what it is. Spilling my guts in front of three hundred people, many of whom are old friends, is intimidating to me. Though I am excited at the prospect, another side of me wants to escape. About three years ago I attended a workshop though the Aspen Writers' Foundation taught by Karen Chamberlain. I remember her saying that everyone has a story to tell, and every family story is important, just as every person is important. As I think about this I regret my cowardice all the more. A few days later Barry calls me back one more time to try to convince me, and I happily acquiesce.

It's such a big topic to cover in ten minutes, but I decide to essentially tell the story of the first chapter of this book and begin by quoting the first paragraph. As the performance date grows near I realize that I can't commit it all to memory, and decide that I'm better off making a brief organizational outline, learning my first paragraph, then winging it from there. I try to forget about it as much as possible and get on with the writing. My daughter was visiting and the day before the performance I decide to try it out on her. It's pretty horrible. I tick off names and dates and it sounds like some cheap travelogue. Tasha tells me it's not working. I have to take another approach. Forget the timeline, describe the people and what I'm doing. List five things I want to put out there, make sure I include them, then hope I can make it flow during the performance. I try that approach in front of my wife the afternoon of the show. It goes better, but I stammer and backtrack, get lost and begin to get fearful again.

The night of the show each of us have a little pizza and salad backstage and try to pretend we aren't nervous. There are some luminaries there including Sheriff Bob Braudis, Clifford Irving, and Barry himself. Bob was Hunter Thompson's best friend, and our gonzo sheriff going on twenty years at this point. Irving is the writer who went to prison for his "unauthorized" Howard Hughes biography, and he's going to talk about his jail time. I eat lightly, drink one glass of white wine, and see that I'm third in the line-up. That's good. Not right at the beginning, but not so long to wait with a belly full of butterflies.

When my turn comes, I walk up to the microphone with a bottle of water and set it on a stool and face the audience. Because I'm not a real tall guy, a friend yells out, "Stand up!" I smile, say "Thank you," and deliver my first paragraph. From then on, I have no idea what happens. It seems to go well. About two-thirds of the way through, my mind goes completely blank for about twenty seconds, but most people read it as an emotional recovery. In fact there are a few audible sobs out there, which in some strange way is gratifying. I am in a daze as people hug me and pass out their compliments in the lobby, but I can't even now begin to reconstruct exactly what I said. It's done, the video is in the can, and someday I'll get to see what happened. It served its purpose—a public commitment to the completion of this task, and I'm glad that I did it.

*

I'm realizing that I need to dig back one more time through Uri's letters from Christmas through January 20th. They are the only ones not in envelopes. I've got them rolled up with rubber bands. This should be the last visit. The story is complete and imprinted, but I just want to get the feel of him one more time. I guess I could go through them all again in my old age, but I don't think I'll need to. He's become tangible. Just yesterday I came across a few of his books I'd forgotten about on an upstairs bookshelf. The small, blue, annotated New Hudson Shakespeare, *As You Like It*, and a similar-sized olive-colored Tennyson collection. He seems to have underlined passages and both are signed on the inside left cover:

Uri A. Munro 1937

That would have been the year he graduated from Dartmouth. I've been a poetry lover since my fourth-grade teacher, mentioned earlier, made us memorize *The Congo* by Vachel Lindsay. Now I have another little project. I'll add these two books to my reading pile next to the bed. I'm Shakespeare ignorant and Tennyson familiar. Maybe his underlining will tell me something. Uri thought enough about these books to sign them and keep them, so I'll try to find out why.

Sometimes I feel like a detective who is investigating himself. I keep thinking that my mother and I should have talked more about him, but it never came easy. Little things surfaced—a few stories from time to time, but that's all. I'm getting a closer look now and it isn't over yet.

I probably could have matched some of the letters with the envelopes but somehow they've become separated. I'm pretty sure that he was sending three or four letters per envelope and it's probably easier to keep them rolled up.

As I read the letters again I'm reminded of my son's easy banter. He and Uri seem like peas in a pod. I know that Mary Lynn has a few dozen of my shipboard letters tucked away. I will read them soon just to get another cross-correlation. Maybe I was more like my father and my son at that age than I remember. Now, I'm not so innocent. Somehow that's how my dad strikes me—innocent. I am starting to recognize myself more and more in him. Just his sense of the personal—his use of time. His frame of mind is my own. Paradoxically he's always referring to Mom as "old girl," which sounds strange to me. As I look at my grandfather's scrapbooks I realize that Alec raised Uri a good and proper Ivy Leaguer, but with a British overlay. Photos show Uri and Alec beside flashy convertibles, or dressed fashionably for tennis or golf. With my grandmother Varvara, they lounge around deck pools on ocean liners, pose on old wooden skis, or relax at the beach.

*

Uri is flying combat missions almost daily this second week in January, and the letters reflect his energy level. Like everyone else on board, he's tired and he knows there's a long cruise ahead of him. It's going to be one battle after another with little chance of a break. The TBM, like any prop-driven warplane, was a noisy, stress-inducing machine. If you've ever watched actual aerial combat or air attack footage, you can imagine the intensity in the cockpit. If you weren't strapped tightly by your shoulder harness, your helmet would be bouncing off the canopy. Add the adrenalin surges and g-forces to the irregular hours and you see why cruises were scheduled from four to six months maximum duration. If all goes well, he'll get two or three weeks leave in the early summer before returning to his squadron.

> *Today was a tragic day for the fighters. They sent out two*
> *four plane patrols to strike the Hong Kong and Canton area*
> *and they got back about nine o'clock this evening. The first one*
> *to land crashed the barrier and flopped onto his back. The pilot*
> *was OK. The second flew into the water astern of the ship and*

exploded, without signs of a survivor [ENS Erwin G. Nash].
Another barrier crash. The fourth was a wheels-up landing.
A fifth is still missing with no trace or clue [LT(jg) Robert F.
Wright]. It was one of those frightfully unlucky days that makes
a person stop and wonder if this aviation business is entirely
practical after all and especially at night.
— from Hadley's VT(N)-90 squadron history

I'm digging one more time into the last few letters, then will re-read Hadley's chronicle and the pertinent parts of *The Big E* one more time too. Uri is streaming together pages written on consecutive days since mail might only leave the ship every week or so.

January 18th

There isn't too much to report about the time spent aboard ship. The weather continues to pound them all and Uri wonders how the boys on the smaller ships can handle it.

This afternoon there were funeral services for Bob Brought,
one of Hedden's crewmen. He was seriously injured in the deck
crash which pulled their plane apart near the tail a few days ago
and died early this morning. This was our first burial at sea.

The service was held on the fantail with the heaving,
tumultuous sea of blue and white as a background. The other
ships of the force were visible and groups of planes returning
from day strikes and patrols roared overhead. The sky was gray
and laden with dark clouds, and the noise of the sea drowned
out the words of the chaplain as he paid simple tribute to our
young shipmate and friend who had given his life for our cause.
Then the Chaplain, reading the burial-at-sea service, came to the
words, "I commit this body to the deep... ." The stretcher was
tilted up and the body slid from beneath the flag into the depths
of the ocean. The Marine guard fired a salute as Taps was
sounded. The band played "Onward Christian Soldiers" as we
sadly left the fantail and went to our several tasks.
— from Hadley's VT(N)-90 squadron history

A good part of the flight crew's time is spent sleeping and eating in order to sustain the round-the-clock operations. Uri's handwriting is large now and he's numbering the letters on the outside so that she can read them in "some sort of logical sequence." He's been playing bridge with some of the new officers who have joined the squadron. He's won a few bucks and will add the winnings to the money order he sends her from each paycheck. He's still eating Christmas candy and fruitcake, but comments that, "If you were here my dear, with your little appetite, it wouldn't last two days though!"

January 19th

Uri had strong hopes of getting mail today, but no luck. Now I know that he's already read his last letters from Betsy. All that she mailed after January 2nd were forwarded back to her in the months ahead. He mentions the lack of mail.

> I'm very much afraid that I won't even get a smell of it for at least a week now. Too bad.

> We have a nice little wardroom pantry near the ready room, and when we are up at night we can always go in and get a cocoa or coffee, and toast, peanut butter or jelly, and tonight a plate of cold chicken to make chicken sandwiches with. Really a very nice little set-up from any point of view. I'm not a great eater, as you know, and I don't think of food before anything else, but it's still pretty nice to have – and all free! That must be what really appeals to me!

Here my father sounds like my son, Alex, again. The last letter I have been able to find is dated January 20th. Again, nothing is out of the ordinary. He's mailing a money order for seventy dollars home with instructions to sock it away for his little "would be Scotchman."

> ... that includes every cent I have at present. Don't sock it all away though. I want you to take whatever you want of it and get yourself a present from me. Maybe cute pajamas, or a cute white nightgown, or something else you want. It will be an anniversary present from me for that lucky day in my life when we walked out of the

church into that beautiful snowstorm, and I knew once and for all I had you where I wanted you, and that was right by my side for the rest of our lives together. That, and all that goes with it and all that it means, has been the turning point of my life. Until tomorrow my love, so long –

Uri

Those are almost the last words Betsy would read. There is one more letter, nothing special, just a few newsy items.

January 20, 1945

I'm going to try and write at least two letters a day here while I can, then I'll be in pretty good shape as far as letter writing goes.

Speaking of shapes, recalls yours to me darling – and it is perfection itself, its sole drawback being that it is too far away. However well I remember that shape, I still intend to get firmly re-acquainted with it, and diligently on the next opportunity. So take heed, and lady beware.

Your loving,
Uri

*

Should I have expected more from these letters? Maybe I was hoping to gain deep insights as he revealed his innermost thoughts from sixty-three years ago. His comments on the war effort are brief, and I have already included them in these pages. Censorship made so much of it impossible to talk about, and what could he say really? There was little time for introspection. There wasn't much to consider about the war other than doing the job in front of you each day and praying it would end soon.

By this time, there is little doubt as to the outcome of the war. It's a matter of forcing things through to their conclusion, and there are still plenty of risks to be taken. For a few days, flights are cancelled because of bad weather. During the respite, many of the flight crews have been studying Spanish with Ed Hildago, who just made lieutenant. He grew up speaking Spanish, and the whole crew is impressed by his teaching skills. Uri covers the daily events briefly, but of course the letters are mostly endearments. They're feeling close to each other, and I'm fortunate to be a part of it again at this time in my life.

I also have access to the *Enterprise* unofficial website and journals, but there aren't any detailed entries or background material relating to the attacks on Formosa that took place on January 20–22. I was hoping to find action reports and flight logs for those night attacks, but so far no luck. On the map though, it's easy to spot Kiirun Harbor on the northwest coast of Taiwan. It is called Keelung Harbor now, and its wide mouth is navigable for ten miles to the south before the river narrows. It would be helpful to find pictures of the harbor as it existed in 1945. Now the entire area into the surrounding hills is a maze of overlapping Taiwanese cities.

The day of Uri's last letter, the action was accelerating. Several incoming bogeys—unidentified aircraft—were picked up on ship's radar, and all but one were shot down before they were in sight of the task force. The lone intruder was "splashed" before he could endanger any ship, but it marked the first time since its Christmas departure that the ship had been forced to defend itself. The next day, January 21, found the crew rising early to the General Quarters alarm. The word spread that the ship was under air attack, but soon it was announced that all of the incoming aircraft had been shot down by ships defending the perimeter of the force. It turned out that most of the planes shot down had been even farther away. All but one were Japanese transports evacuating Luzon.

F6F HELLCAT COMING ABOARD

Now the squadron is fully engaged and preparing for a substantial night attack on Kiirun Harbor. It's the largest harbor complex on the island—eighteen huge cargo ships were seen there only yesterday. Aircrews have been getting briefings about Formosa. They were warned that if shot down, not to expect help from the local population. Both the Americans and Japanese are despised, and contact should be avoided. No matter. This is the first attack on substantial shipping targets for the torpedo boys and they're anxious to get on with it. Intelligence indicates that the enemy is loading up transports in the harbor under the prevailing low cloud cover during the day. The ships then run along the coast at night to re-supply the southern part of Formosa. Kiirun was a last strategic stronghold and expected to be heavily defended.

Seven Avengers are launched into windy, moonless skies at 0200 hours, January 22nd. Kip is the flight leader, with Uri as his radarman/bombardier, and Airman First Class Paul Floyd manning the turret-mounted fifty-caliber. Lt. Moore, flying the seventh plane, develops radio trouble and lands back aboard, fuming at his bad luck. This leaves two sections of three planes each heading west. The second section is led by Cdr. Bill Martin, leader of the Air Group 90 staff. It is a lengthy two-hour flight to the target. Admiral "Bull" Halsey thinks he has actually finished his role on Formosa and is moving toward dawn strikes on Okinawa and the Nansei Shoto Archipelago. The attack on Kiirun Harbor would cause the Japanese to think that the *Enterprise* and Task Force 38 are still in the immediate area, rather than massing four hundred miles to the east.

*

I've done some loose formation flying at night and it requires full attention. Flying tight is much easier. In close formation you're only a dozen feet away. You fly off your wingman by lining up two reference points on his aircraft with a spot on the inside of your canopy. The lead plane does the navigation as well as indicating all climbs, turns, power changes, and descents with head signals. On an attack, these signals allow the formation to maintain radio silence as it approaches the target. The nice thing about formation flying is that if the leader flies right, you will too. Your job is to maintain your exact wingman position—continuously adding or subtracting throttle to keep the references points aligned. If your leader executes a barrel-roll, and you're flying right, you will too.

On this flight, the torpedo bombers arc in a scouting line—a whole different thing. You're flying on instruments while simultaneously keeping the adjacent plane in sight, hundreds of yards away, through your canopy. Everyone flies off the leader indirectly, but in fact keeps the proper distance from his wingman at all times, who is in turn flying off his own wingman. On a long flight, at night with no horizon, it's easy to become disoriented as you crane your neck looking for your wingmates. The seat of your pants is not a reliable indicator of the levelness of your wings. If you don't keep your attitude gyro (artificial horizon indicator) level, the world can turn on its side, but it will feel perfectly normal. It is important though; on a long flight to the target, the spaced-out scouting line makes you less likely to be detected by ships' radar or enemy aircraft.

*

Each plane carries an extra fuel tank in its second bomb bay, three high-velocity five-inch rockets under each wing, and two 500-pound bombs. They stay above 6,000 feet to clear the clouds, and in two hours the western coast of Formosa begins to appear. Kip tightens up the formation as they turn northeast toward the radar-painted image of Kiirun Harbor. It is much like the situation that Kippen faced at Truk Lagoon eleven months earlier and the strike plan is similar. Martin is a seasoned combat pilot, and as a commander, senior to Lieutenant Kippen, but as a non-squadron member is assigned command of the second division.

> *Kiirun was socked in as advertised. Heavy broken clouds hung low over the harbor and extended up to 5,000 or 6,000 feet. Above that the sky was clear and the visibility was good. Kippen and his first section headed immediately for the initial point, five miles north of the harbor entrance. Martin circled out on a sweep to the north and west for any shipping that might have recently left the harbor.*
>
> — Edward P. Stafford, *The Big E*, p. 493

The "initial point" is the rendezvous location from which each pilot would begin his attack. Aircraft depart this point at predetermined intervals and zip into the outer harbor down low on the water in order to avoid the anti-aircraft batteries. Ships in the outer harbor are being hit first, and until they're disposed of, no one is to enter the inner harbor. As leader, Kip is first off the perch, and it soon becomes apparent that the enemy is not taken by surprise. Searchlights race through the clouds, and tracers streak upwards from all over the harbor entrance as the guns open up. Bill Martin leaves his wingmen at the initial point and climbs to 8,000 feet directly above Kip's Avenger. He is acting as a decoy to divert the AA fire while Kip, blinded by searchlights piercing his canopy, twice has to circle back for another try. He dives between hills on the rocky shore, and comes in low for the third time. Martin's plan is working. Fire is being redirected from Kippen's plane as the tracers jump to the higher aircraft. Martin's radioman, Barnett, shoves square bundles of foil "window" through the bomb bay doors. It floats down—further confusing the enemy's fire-control radar.

> *The second hand on Martin's instrument panel moved with tiny jerks around its red-lighted rim. When it was time for Kip*

*to have reached the inner harbor, Martin banked and peered
down at the gun flashes and thick pencils of light rooted in
Kiirun, half hidden by its constant clouds. The red flare of an
explosion erupted in the inner harbor, lighting the clouds and
hills and reflecting in the black water for a second or two before
it contracted to a steady flaming that showed the shape of a big
ship under the shifting fire and smoke. Russ Kippen, calm and
competent as always, had placed his bombs perfectly.*

*Already the second plane of Kip's section was in the outer
harbor, with Martin's second flying decoy 8,000 feet above him,
and the two remaining aircraft had left the initial point inbound,
one high and one low. Martin was turning and losing altitude,
on the way to begin his own run, when a second, smaller, red
flash and a brief fire bloomed against a hillside south of the
harbor.*

— Edward P. Stafford, *The Big E,* p. 494

The attacks continue, and the inner harbor rages from fires set by
the initial hits of Kippen and his first section. Exploding ships and
warehouses send flashing plumes tearing into the dawn pre-light. Am-
munition stored dockside cooks off as the second section climbs to altitude above the target. For an hour they circle there as their fuel gages
move toward empty. No planes from the first section ever joined up,
so Martin reluctantly heads toward the *Enterprise.* As the three planes,
nearly running on fumes, approach the ship, Bill Martin realizes that
the smaller red flash had likely been Kip's plane. He was either shot
down, or unable to pull out of his steep dive toward the hills rising
behind his target.

Here's where the two accounts differ, and I have no way to resolve
them. Stafford's book is considerably more detailed. Hadley's description of the attack is limited to a few paragraphs, written perhaps before all the facts were in. It makes no difference really. Many family
survivors have none of the details, while I pretty much know how it
all happened. I've read the accounts over and over again, studied the
maps and I'm glad to know about it.

*Those pilots who made the attack were Kippen, Koop [LT (jg)
Chester G. Koop], and Wood [ENS John P. Wood] in the
first division and Cmdr. Martin, Jennings, and Cromley in the*

*second division. The planes carried two 500lb bombs and eight
rockets. The round trip established (or close to it) a record for
long-range strikes. Turret navigator Peter Smith reported it was
off his plotting board on the return trip. The plan was for the
first division to attack as soon as they reached the target while the
second division searched along the west coast for shipping targets,
making their attack on the harbor later and after the first division
had completed theirs. In general this plan was carried out:
Kippen made the first run announcing the commencement of his
attack by radio—that was the last ever heard from him. When
the attack started, numerous search lights came on so Cmdr.
Martin returned to the target staying at 6000 feet to act as a
searchlight decoy and cover the attacking planes. Kippen made his
attack on a FTB tied alongside a dock, scoring hits and starting
fires on the shore which spread rapidly, as well as causing the
ship itself to explode. A few minutes later an explosion was
seen near the mouth of the harbor which is now believed to be
Kippen's plane when it hit the water ...*

— from Hadley's VT(N)-90 squadron history

*

When I was at the Naval Academy, I wrote my senior thesis on
the role of the *USS Enterprise* in World War II. I studied the ship for
months, and finished up my research at the Naval Archives in Washington, DC I stayed for an afternoon reading the logs and transcrip-
tions until I came to the battle in which my father was lost. As I read
the radio transmissions, my throat went dry, sweat trickled down my
sides, and I found myself out of breath. There in black and white
were the other pilots' descriptions of my father's plane making its final
bombing run on a warehouse adjoining the docks. Searchlights, tracers, and flares streaked the sky as his plane made its third attack. Now
as I re-read these accounts, that feeling returns. The pilots on the flight
are quoted at length, and the red flash on the hill makes the most sense
in the narration.

And from the next day ...

*We had quite an unusual squadron meeting this evening.
Cmdr. Martin spoke to us concerning yesterday's losses, giving
us his ideas about what happened. He's got a pretty good way
of looking at that sort of thing. Out here (he says) there's a*

job to be done regardless of inevitable misfortune. We expect losses and count on them so that they don't hit us the way they ordinarily would. But we're not hardhearted or cold blooded in this outlook—we've just got too much more to do now—we can't afford to look back or take time for extensive thought. So we have our sincere and deeply heartfelt regrets but shake them off quickly and go on as normally as possible. It's the only way. And later, when we've done our part of the job we'll take care of our sorrows. After the Commander's talk, they did an unprecedented thing. They passed out a ration of brandy, in small bottles with the Navy seal over the top, to the whole squadron. "For medical purposes only," but the Commander got permission to declare a "medical emergency" and the rules were relaxed. Doc (Lt. Comdr.) Hurlburt [Edwin G. Hurlburt] issued a blanket prescription. It was two ounce slugs per man but that little bit was mighty potent and was well received by all hands.

— from Hadley's VT(N)-90 squadron history

Betsy

I've already read most of Mom's letters that were written after Kiirun Harbor. I've already quoted the one she wrote on February 7, before she knew he was missing, and would have to go back to her earlier letter of January 22 to put the two of them together on his last day. Going back to it now, it's a happy, flirty letter—the one where I kept telling everyone how "fart" they were. It probably doesn't make any sense to do this. In some way I'm groping for a sense of the supernatural, while everything that I believe tells me otherwise. I search both of their letters leading up to Kiirun Harbor for some sign, but of course she had no way of knowing that about the time she was going to sleep, Uri was rolling out of his rack for his 2 a.m. launch. This time juxtaposition is an illusion caused by the uncertainty and lag in mail deliveries. They're responding to each other based on letters written weeks earlier, which conveys a surreal overlay.

This is where part of the story ends. It's two-and-one-half weeks since Kiirun Harbor, and I close up Mom's letter as soon as I realized what it is. There are only two more letters that I know of. She may have continued writing, but where would she have sent them? All of her most recent letters have been returned, including these last two. I have to brace myself. It means that I will hold off for just a little while before reading.

I keep wondering if I'm exploiting my parents by revealing so much of their intimacy. They're both gone now, but unexpectedly at this time in my life they've given me the opportunity to tell their story. It has caused me to consider my mother in a way that I would never have expected, and finally to feel like I spent some time with my dad. Even more, it's the idea of their relationship. The loss of my father was always there in front of Mom and I can see now the underlying sadness that made her tough and determined—but vulnerable.

February 8, 1945

My Dearest Darling,

Married four years ago today Uri. Four years married is quite a length of time but this five months of separation seems twice as long. I love you more than you'll ever know darling and as I've said many times before I live only for the day when we're together again.

Today we received the telegram saying that you are missing in action. That changes none of my plans for the future as I don't believe it and won't. I'll admit that I feel like hell, and shakey as the dickens because I could be wrong but I don't think I am.

Our constant thoughts are with you as always. I've never stopped thinking of you one minute since I waved goodbye to you in San Diego. Thinking of you is my main happiness because you are the source of all the happiness that I've even really known. Wouldn't it be wonderful if we could go back to that night, or for that matter to go back to any time when we were together. As I've said before, I'll never be fool enough not to make the most of our lives together, living and enjoying each day as it comes.

Uri I'll admit that it's tough writing tonight under the strain of that telegram. No sense in lying to you because you know me well enough to know that I couldn't be happy right now. When you receive this you will know that I know that all is well. It must have been hell for you too knowing that we feared for you while you knew that you were safe.

Goodnight my darling.

I love you,
Betsy

Now her last letter is coming up. I can hardly stand to read it. I'll have to wait until later to gather my thoughts. She's refusing to accept it, because if it's true, she believes that her life is over. She mentions future letters, but I don't think there were any more. If so, she didn't mail them or I'd have them here somewhere. I'm learning that despite the next sixty-two years of her life, and a wonderful second marriage, that no one could ever replace Uri. This was confirmed to me later by Vandy Bauer, her best friend. Uri was all of the love that she had to give in the deepest sense of things. From here on, part of her would be missing, and I have to think that through.

I woke up at two thirty last night and couldn't get back to sleep. Did Mom keep the letters all those years so that one day I would have them? I'm starting to doubt that. It seems more likely that she just couldn't bear to throw them away. Her final two letters, written after she got the February 7th telegram, were the last stand. She was refusing to accept him as missing. She couldn't imagine him not surviving, not being out there somewhere. The last letter ended with, "I love you,

I love you, I love you, I love you, I love you", over and over again written across the bottom of the page. It was all she could say. It was her way to keep him alive.

Saturday, February 10, 1945

It's hard writing just now but I shall try my best. No sense in trying to fool you Uri, my heart is broken but I have all the hope in the world. I know that nothing can happen to my Uri. The folks are being very brave and together we're making the best of it. The day that we know you are safe will be the happiest of all our lives. In future letters I'm not going to refer to your missing in any way, first because I don't think of you that way and second it's an awful thought however you look at it. Uri I love you so very very much, if I am wrong and you are really gone life is over with me for many reasons. I could list them but you know them as well as I do. The reasons are all you and things to do with you. I can't write about it even Uri, the many thoughts connected with the whole thing has me so confused. When you read this just remember I love you, I love you, I love you. Nothing else means a thing to me. Just to hear the word that you are safe will make me the happiest person in this world even if I know that I must wait years before I see you.

Mother's called me twice and Fred

Jenkin called. I've had letters from Bernie, Bert Bradshaw and Mrs. Whitlock (lives here in Harbor Heights, one of her sons is missing.) Mother says that many people have called and been to the house — ah Uri, Uri, you must be safe. It can't be any other way. In a few days I shall probably be able to write a better letter. Now I just can't do it. All that I can do is hope and pray with all the strength I have that you are all right.

> Goodnight my dearest,
> darling Uri.
> I love you,
> Betsy

Uri my letter sounds so dumb I should not even mail it, but oh God how my heart aches — if I wrote how I felt you would dive over board after reading it.

I love you, I love you, I love you, I love you, I love you...

Since these two letters had never been opened, it seemed like it was happening for me as it was happening for her. It was as if *just now* she was discovering Uri was missing. Now her whole life is going to hit me in a different way. I could almost breathe her when I opened the February 9th letter. It didn't happen sixty-four years ago—but just this instant. And what did she tell me as a little boy when I woke up the next morning in Greenwich? When did I begin to understand what had happened? And how did not having my father in my life affect me? I don't really have any memories of finding out that he was lost, but it must have altered me in some way. There's an underlying insecurity. Maybe we all have that inside of us, but for me I now know that something was missing. I'm my father's boy after all. He lives inside

142

of me as he has all along, but I couldn't feel it before. That's what's so important, and why being given the letters has changed me. I wish that I could talk with my mother about this, but we'd both just cry our eyes out. I'm her boy too.

*

Where do I go from here? It may not be important, but for a long time I've felt a need to go to Russia. I want to see what the country-side is like around St. Petersburg, and to spend enough time to rub my nose in it a little. Maybe there are some remaining threads of my grandmother's Gansin family. But it's unlikely that would lead any-where. Who would remember stories of a White Russian woman who escaped her country ninety-four years earlier? More tangibly, I'd like to go to Taiwan and walk around Kiirun Harbor, just to be in that place. I've spent hours looking it over from satellite photos. There are some things that will never be finished unless I touch these bases.

It's all part of a broader picture that needs to be internalized. There is a picture somewhere of Uri's gravestone in the American National Cemetery in Manila. I saw it once and now I can't find it anywhere. I guess it wouldn't be impossible to pass by the Philippines on the way back from Kiirun, even though I know he was never buried there. I'd see his name, rank, and the state of Connecticut carved in marble with January 22, 1945 on the last line. The cemetery drapes a hill-side meadow with countless curved rows of white crosses. Am I seeing snowcapped mountains as well as the Pacific in the distance at the cemetery's website? I've resolved to have a photograph taken of the carving, or perhaps have someone do a tracing.

The writing process has created an underlying reverence for my whole concept of family that goes beyond anything I expected. I have tried to honor my parents' dreams by connecting them to all of us who come after. Now my grandchildren will know Betsy, Uri, and Alec. They too will have a story to tell.

I just went through the credenza. It's our family photo cabinet, full of images from the late '60s until the digital age. They're mostly slides, but I was hoping to find some more photographs of Uri and Betsy. No luck. The next step would be to contact my family to see if anything else turned up when the house was cleared out. Things fell apart with her husband Ted and the family about a year after Mom died. There was a dispute over her house and the landscaping business Ted and my brother Joe had built together. I feel lucky that Ted took the time to mail me the box of letters. I don't even have a telephone number for him to see if there could be anything else. It could be close to the end of the memorabilia trail. But there is one more reading session ahead of me—a quick look again at Uri's last letters and a small pile of condolences.

Now I've been through the letters, probably for the last time. I don't think that I should ever need to see them again, but they're in the lockbox for the next member of our family who may someday be curious. As I pull out the letters to my mother from Uri's squadron mates, I'm surprised by their thickness. There are only seven letters, but some are three or four pages long. I have been waiting to hear anyone speak personally about Uri, and this may be the last chance. He isn't mentioned meaningfully in the Hadley squadron chronicle, so I haven't had a chance to see him in the context of his shipmates. A squadron is a tight family, pulled close by the shared mission, as well as the shared losses. I went out last night to play music, but kept thinking about this last little pile of envelopes.

The first letter, from Lieutenant Jim Plummer, was mailed to Betsy less than a month and a half after Kiirun. He sat down to write the letter after receiving a letter she had written to him. I wish now that I had that letter as well. Jim writes in beautiful, flowing, ruled script, brown ink on tan paper:

March 2, 1945

> *I am not able to tell you exactly where we were attacking that day, but I can say that it was a very heavily defended stronghold of the enemy. Uri, as he had on many previous missions, was flying with our skipper, Lt. R. F. Kippen. The attack was before sunrise, and it was partially Uri's skill which took the section safely to the target. The section arrived at the target at the prescribed time and the various planes peeled off to make their individual attacks. The last word heard from Uri's plane was when the skipper announced that he was commencing his attack. That is all that is known definitely. The other pilots saw a fire which could have been their plane but might just as well have been one of the others, or a bomb hit on the ground. No one saw the fire close enough to be sure what it was.*

I personally think that there is a very good chance that some, if not all, of the plane's crew could survive the crash. We have had similar crashes near our forces in which all of the members came out in fine shape.

We can only hope and pray that Uri did survive the crash in the water and was taken prisoner.

Uri did a very fine job in training the men of the squadron in our operational tactics. His efforts have been instrumental in causing the enemy a great many setbacks. He was liked by all members of the squadron and we all felt his absence deeply.

Sincerely,
Jim Plummer

As was common in the service, Uri had designated a squadron mate to arrange his effects, and he chose Jim Plummer. Jim gathered everything and mailed it to Betsy when he returned to the States. His last sentence is perhaps more true that he realized ...

... I think that they may mean a lot to your son in future years.

I have Uri's officer's cap, a few other uniform items, and his medals, which likely were sent to my mother later.

The next letter is from Alma Kippen, the skipper's mother. I had to read it three times. She meanders with emotion, but it adds meaningfully to the picture. She too is responding to a letter from Betsy, who must have been contacting anyone she could for information.

April 21, 1945

Dear Mrs. Munro,

Your letter arrived this noon. I am so pleased to hear from you. also to know that you had so much trust in Russell. that is why I can't figure out why he did not return.

... my only hope is that they are any where, and are wounded. One can look out for the other one. that is some consolation. it's not that I want anyone to be missing or any harm come to any one for I worried so much since the war was on and this last three months I have gone through hell. I can't eat or sleep and

lost about 20 lbs. I am a wreck and I know how you and Mrs. Floyd feel.

… I only hope that they are on an island, or even if they were in a prison camp there may be a chance, if only we knew, we could send them food. I imagine the Japs will starve them. Russell was so thin. he will collapse if he don't get food.

… please excuse this bad writing as I can't keep a steady hand since this happened. bye bye.

Alma Kippen

In the letter from May 5th there is another little mystery to unravel. The first three-fourths of the page is signed by Lt. William D. Bacon, Torpedo Ninety's administrative officer. It is addressed to Mrs. Floyd, the mother of Airman First Class Paul Floyd who was the tail gunner and third crewman on the flight. Bacon again describes the attack for her:

In the early morning of January 22nd an attack was made on Kiirun Harbor, Formosa. Lt. Kippen's plane was seen to make an effective low level attack causing severe damage to Japanese installations and was not heard from thereafter. It was impossible to tell exactly what happened for it was completely dark and a moonless night. I believe you will appreciate my frankness though when I say, with much regret, that we do not entertain any hope of their survival.

On the bottom fourth of the page, and continuing to the other side is another letter addressed to "My Dear Mrs. Floyd." The handwriting is identical, but is signed by Lt. Charles Henderson. Perhaps one of the two officers copied the letter for the other. Lt. Henderson apologizes for the information arriving so slowly to Mrs. Floyd.

We have lost two skippers, and I am the third. We just came in and I received your letter of March 19th.

Frankly I could happily crucify the people responsible for your not having received the details of your tragic loss. Mrs. Kippen, the mother of our 1st skipper, and Paul's pilot, suffered in the same manner.

... However I shall give you the details in the event that you have not received the letters forwarded by our ship's chaplain.

... Kip led a flight against shipping in Kiirun Harbor, N. Formosa on Jan. 22nd. They took off about midnight in foul weather, 200 miles east of the target, 6 planes.

He attacked first, a low level bombing run. Searchlights and anti-aircraft were intense. He made a transmission,—"I am going in now" and shortly thereafter there was a large explosion and fires, on the edge of the docks, and among adjacent warehouses. He had scored a direct hit on a large ship. He was not heard from again and the other pilots are certain that his plane hit an obstruction or was hit by AA and that one of the fires was his plane.

Had they survived the attack, contact would have been made.

I know how you have suffered and wish that, in some way, I could help you. Let me take one passage from a letter which we received from Mrs. Collins. Her husband, our 2nd skipper, was shot down one month later by our own forces.

... "Thank you for being frank—there is no sense in avoiding the blows that are awaiting you when there is no way to alter your fate—therefore—the sooner one can face life in the eye and still decide it's worth living, the better off one is. I am so very glad that I met Bud's shipmates, and those two glorious weeks in San Diego where the whole squadron was together will always live in my memory. I am not bitter because it was chalked up to come out this way from the day each of us was born—I was lucky to be his wife and bear his child—If he had to die for us—now, I have to live for him."

I thought that the only tears I would shed would come from my parents' letters, but this one got me too. It made me realize that there was a need to include it, along with the other condolences. I stopped reading Hadley's chronicle after January 22nd, but now it makes sense to read on. The story of Torpedo 90's first and last attack cruise is far from over. I had no idea about Lt. Collins' death, but his wife's elegance under stress is undeniable. She gave birth to his son three weeks later.

It's time to get out from under the weight of all this. The process has served its purpose. It's possible that I'm overstating the case for Mom's experience of her loss. After all, she went on to have a big family, surrounded herself with lifelong friends, and was married to a good man for thirty-seven years, and after his death, married once again. She became involved in politics and controversy, raised five kids, and maintained her energy and humor. But this story is set in a time when none of this had yet happened. For now, Uri was the father of her only son, and like the millions of others who suffered losses, she never got over him. But it doesn't mean she didn't carry on. I've said that it made her tougher, and the rest of her life made that apparent. She was strong, but with an underlying sadness that we could all sense.

Ten years ago I called her when my daughter Natasha had her first child. It was a crystalline Sunday morning in March when I rang her from Colorado. I asked if she was ready to cry a little. She had a beautiful great-grandson—his name was Uri.

End

Epilogue

Each of my four grandchildren knew their great-grandmother Betsy. And although later they will likely have faint memories of her, they knew only the eighty-year-old version. She could still command the evening in any room—telling stories, laughing, drinking (although not as much in her later years) and smoking (though we'd driven her to the porch by this time). In those last years she often decided to quit, but never did so for more than a day or two. She lived in a cloud of smoke, and you could see that it was slowing her down. Looking back, it was a thread of continuity—the only thing she had all those years that stayed the same. She absolutely loved her cigarettes. Still, she was more than the sum of her parts, and all of her parts were churning along, even in those final years.

In October 1948, Mom married Bob "Steve" Stephens, who was attending Ohio State on the G.I. Bill. Steve had been an Army captain, a paratrooper in the 82nd Airborne. He fought in the Battle of the Bulge and later served in the occupational forces in Germany. He was a good-natured, fair and honest man. Together they had two more boys, Mike and Joe, and also adopted a boy, Bobby, and our sister, Nancy. We became a family of five kids—all treated the same.

In the late 1980s, my stepfather Steve died from heart problems. It was a sad period for all of us. It wasn't long before Betsy was ready to leave Florida, where they had moved to in the early '70s. She was in love with the mountains, as I knew from our car trips back and forth between Maryland and Ohio in the late 1940s. We had this great two-tone tan Chevy coupe, and we would sing our hearts out as Route 40 climbed through the mountains of West Virginia. A few years before Steve died, he and Betsy bought a little cabin on a mountainside in rural North Carolina. When he was gone, she sold the house in Sebring and moved to the very top of nearby Smokerise Mountain outside of Hayesville. In 1997 she married one more time. She called Ted Williams her "diamond in the rough," and they had almost ten years together.

She was a popular figure on her rural mountaintop. She made friends with neighbors, drove miles at night to teach bridge, and got involved with most everyone she met. She was always giving away her possessions to people she hardly knew. She donated to the less fortunate there in the hills, babysat their kids, and visited the old folks at their homes or in the hospitals. Years before, in Florida, she spent weekends teaching handicapped kids to swim. Everyone loved the feisty old blonde with the raspy voice and energy enough for all. She had an overriding affection for the underdog and hated injustice and prejudice of any kind. I believe now that her loss of Uri nurtured that soft spot in her heart. Emotionally attracted to causes, she was always engaging her friends and neighbors in local issues. Perhaps for the same reason, she was hot tempered and sometimes it was smart to stay away from her until she cooled off.

At the end she fooled us. We had been warning her of lung cancer for years, and it would have been the greatest humiliation for her to be diagnosed. A few months before her eighty-sixth birthday, and two days after some medical tests, she seemed depressed. She said she was tired, and went to bed early. That night she had a heart attack in her bed. There was no chance to tell us about the cancer. It all happened at once, and we were thankful that she never had to admit that it finally got her. More to the point, she never had to confront the ravages that would have followed. She was ready to go, and her timing was perfect.

Acknowledgements

I would first thank my friend and writer/editor in Rostock, Germany: Karl Brehmer. It was at his urging, after reading my first chapter, that I took this project seriously. Three other good friends and writers, Kurt Brown of the Aspen Writers' Conference, Paul Andersen and Morgan Stinemetz, read early manuscripts and I most appreciate their encouragement.

I began in earnest when my wife, Mary Lynn, undertook the epic task of hiking the Appalachian Trail from Georgia to Maine, non-stop, in 2008. Upon her return, after six-and-one-half months, I had completed a rough draft, which she marked up most thoughtfully. Her continuing input as a sounding board helped me eliminate and focus.

My publisher, George Stranahan, with his team at People's Press, gave me the biggest compliment of all when he read my first chapter and said right away that he wanted to publish the book. His total commitment to my absolute freedom, from the very beginning, made the project a joy. Catherine Lutz did a thorough final edit and taught me the joys of *Track Changes*. Craig Wheeless, of Rainy Day Designs, did a wonderful job in the layout and cover, and was a pleasure to work with.

Profound thanks are in order for the read-throughs by Brooke Newman and Clifford Irving (who also did an early edit). Their suggestions, as experienced authors, were timely and indispensable. That they each took the time is unbelievable.

Most importantly, I wish to acknowledge and praise the dedicated contribution of my editor, Karen Chamberlain. A few years before this project began, I took a weekend memoir-writing workshop from Karen, who began directing the Aspen Writers' Foundation in 1985. At the time, and before I received the letters, I shared my ideas with her, and she told me to stay in touch with her when I was ready to start.

This past year found us side by side at my dining room table, in day-long editing sessions. I'd incorporate, and we'd do it again. Then we'd email ideas back and forth and discuss them on the telephone. Karen was suffering those last two sessions, more than I realized, but she was absolutely determined to finish the project. She kept the overview in mind, jostling paragraphs from one chapter to another, and delivered firm but gentle ideas about fixing weaknesses. She unexpectedly passed away only a day after going through the epilogue of this book. She will always be with me—every time I sit down to write.

A special thank you to Betty Hadley, wife of Torpedo Squadron 90's chronicler, Lt. (jg) Robert H. Hadley, who invited us into her home in September 2010 and permitted us to use her husband's journals. Edward P. Stafford's book, *The Big E*, was a primary background source, and I'm most appreciative of the quotes provided.

I'm grateful for my ongoing wonderful relationship with Louise Munro and her most touching letter about Grandpa Alec. Lastly, I have to thank my father and mother, Uri and Betsy, who propelled this project from beginning to end. Without their letters, the families that follow would never know.

Sandy Munro

Glossary

ASP	anti-submarine patrol
attitude gyro	artificial horizon indicator (determines levelness of wings and nose "attitude" – up or down – for instrument flying)
The Big E	*USS Enterprise* nickname
bogey	unidentified aircraft
BOQ	bachelor officers' quarters
cannibalize	to use parts from one aircraft (vehicle/ship) to repair/outfit another
CAP	combat air patrol
CV-6	designation of *USS Enterprise* (aircraft carrier number 6)
CVE	aircraft carrier escort (smaller carrier)
CV(N)-6	*Enterprise* designation beginning December 24th, 1944. (N) denotes "Night"
EOT	engine order telegraph (to send engine commands from bridge to engine room)
F6F	Hellcat fighter aircraft built by Grumman
flattop	aircraft carrier
FTB	dockside repair ship
HAL-3	Helicopter Light Attack Squadron 3
knots	nautical miles (2,000 yards) per hour
light-carrier	smaller supplemental aircraft carrier built upon light-cruiser hull
Nansei Shoto	southern Japanese island group (includes Ryukyu Islands and Okinawa)
ops	operations, as in flight ops
radar/navigator	aircrewman who operates radar and navigation equipment and possibly armaments
Secondary Con	alternative location of all ship controls for command in event of bridge damage

snafu	military jargon for "situation normal, all fucked up"
SNJ	single engine Navy trainer (Texan)
task force	a variety of ships under common command
TBF	Grumman Avenger used as fighter
TBM	Grumman Avenger used as torpedo bomber
TBM-1D	all-weather/night designated version of TBM
USNR	US Naval Reserve
Very pistol	emergency flare pistol
VT(N)-90	Night Torpedo Squadron 90
VF(N)-90	Night Fighter Squadron 90
VT-10	Torpedo Squadron Ten (predecessor to VT(N)-90 aboard Enterprise)
window (foil)	large sheets of tinfoil used to reflect radar signals (to confuse enemy radar)
z-out	sleep, or catnap

US Naval Officer Rankings

Ensign – ENS
Lieutenant Junior Grade – LTJG
Lieutenant – LT
Lieutenant Commander – LCDR
Commander – CDR
Captain – CAPT
Rear Admiral Lower Half – RDML (1 star)
Rear Admiral Upper Half – RADM (2 stars)
Vice Admiral – VADM (3 stars)
Admiral – ADM (4 stars)
Fleet Admiral – wartime only (5 stars)

Photo Credits

All photos printed with permission of source.

Cover	Fighter plane over Pacific Ocean, WWII — Time & Life Pictures/Getty Images
p. 10	Uri Alexander Munro — US Navy photo
p. 50	VT(N)-90 — US Navy photo
p. 63	Arming a TBM Avenger with the Mark 13 torpedo — US Naval Institute photo
p. 116	*The Big E* under dive bomber attack in the Battle of Santa Cruz — US Naval Institute photo
p. 132	F6F Hellcat coming aboard — US Naval Institute photo
all others	Munro family photographs

About the Author

The author lives with his wife Mary Lynn
in the mountains of Colorado.

He can be reached through his Facebook page
or at www.PeoplesPress.org